MASTERS AT WORK

ALSO AVAILABLE

MASTERS AT WORK

BECOMING AN INTERIOR DESIGNER

KATE BOLICK

SIMON & SCHUSTER

New York   London   Toronto   Sydney   New Delhi

Simon & Schuster
1230 Avenue of the Americas
New York, NY 10020

First Simon & Schuster hardcover edition January 2021

SIMON & SCHUSTER and colophon are registered trademarks of
Simon & Schuster, Inc.

For information about special discounts for bulk purchases,
please contact Simon & Schuster Special Sales at 1-866-506-1949
or business@simonandschuster.com

The Simon & Schuster Speakers Bureau can bring authors to your live event. For
more information or to book an event contact the Simon & Schuster Speakers
Bureau at 1-866-248-3049 or visit our website at www.simonspeakers.com.

Manufactured in the United States of America

1   3   5   7   9   10   8   6   4   2

Library of Congress Cataloging-in-Publication Data is available.

ISBN 978-1-9821-3883-7
ISBN 978-1-9821-3884-4 (ebook)

To all of my beloved fellow former *DOMINOS*,
especially Dara Caponigro, whose wisdom
only begins with design

CONTENTS

BECOMING AN
INTERIOR DESIGNER

1

Several moments ago, it was an otherwise ordinary Monday at the offices of Jesse Parris-Lamb, if unseasonably humid for Brooklyn in June. The founders of this residential interior design firm, Amanda Jesse and Whitney Parris-Lamb, had been crouched on the floor, poring over a series of computer printouts of images of chairs and tables, shuffling them around like playing cards, looking for the just-right combination. Every so often one of the two would leap up to pull another image from the folder on the table beside them and introduce it to the mix. They were in the early stages of designing a two-story home library in Connecticut, and the folder contained the results of months of scouting and sourcing ideas. Now it was almost game time: by the end of the following day, they needed to overnight the client a packet of images of their final selections for furnishings and lighting, as well as paint swatches and fabric samples, in preparation for their final meeting the following week.

To a layperson such as me, it was impossible to detect any rhyme or reason to the options spread out on the floor: a pair of pale-pink wingback chairs, a wooden chair with a green seat and a tall windowpane back, a pair of low-slung armchairs in beige, a klismos side chair covered in rust-colored velvet. As someone who writes often about design, I know how to describe what I'm seeing, but actually pulling together all those disparate elements to create a space that's beautiful, comfortable, functional, and original requires abilities that are many leagues beyond me. For a few minutes I tried to imagine myself into the minds of Amanda and Whitney, to see what they were seeing, and failed. (Who wouldn't want to live with every single one of these beautiful chairs? I'll take them all, thank you!)

Then Whitney walked away and returned with a rug sample. The large square of tufted beige wool depicted the head of a giant black-and-brown snake, mouth open wide, seizing what looked like an orange jellyfish between its spiky jaws. Was that a green leaf also sticking out of the jellyfish? I couldn't see what the snake had to do with anything else arrayed before us.

When I expressed my bafflement, Amanda called out to Neala Jacobs, their studio director, at her desk across the room and asked her to find the image they'd been using as inspiration. Neala has been working at Jesse Parris-Lamb (JPL, for short) for only two years, but she's so seamlessly woven into Whitney and Amanda's dynamic that it feels as if she'd been there since day one, five years ago. Neala found the image, printed it out, and walked over to hand it to me.

They'd originally found the image on Pinterest—a reliable source of gorgeously designed living spaces for ideas and inspiration. ("That Pinterest is the backbone of our image sourcing is the dumbest thing," Amanda said, rolling her eyes. "I prefer when we're paging through actual books. But Pinterest provides such an easy way to collect images and share them with the office internally.") The image was of a dining room, not a library, with bare dark-brown wooden floorboards laid down in a chevron pattern, and a pale wooden pedestal table at center paired with midcentury-style molded-plastic hunter-green chairs. Long kelly-green drapes hung at the window, and a pitch-black ceiling light with three long, thin ectomorphic arms hung above all of it, like the most graceful of arachnids. The room was lovely, but I couldn't see what it had to do with the images I was looking at on the floor. Reptilian refinement? Elegance with an edge?

While I was trying to puzzle through their creative process, Whitney's smartphone buzzed, and she answered it. She walked out of the room and into the hallway they use as a concept board, then walked back out into the studio, then back into the hallway again—quickly. Back and forth. Full-on pacing. Amanda began to look concerned.

Head lowered, ear pressed to her phone, Whitney was speaking in a gracious, confident tone that completely belied her obvious anxiety. Tall and rangy, she wears her wavy brown hair in a short crop, which, as she paced, fell over her forehead, obscuring her eyes. As she paced, she looked anywhere but at Amanda—at the floor, at the ceiling. Amanda, unable to read her business partner's expression, returned to her desk, where she sat still as a mouse, and seemed to be doing her best to absorb the contents of the call through osmosis. Across the room, Neala worked quietly at her computer, oblivious of the drama silently unfolding behind her.

Since joining forces to found their firm in 2014, when they were in their early thirties, Whitney and Amanda have amassed an impressive client list of successful executives and artists across all creative fields, from the founder of OkCupid to a famous novelist or three. Along the way, they've developed the communication habits of a long-married couple. They are nearly always together, and when they're not, they are talking on the phone or texting. When they are together but for whatever reason can't speak directly—because one of the duo is locked in a delicate telephone conversation, for instance—they rely on various nonverbal methods, whether reading each other's body language or simply hazarding educated guesses. As I'd come to see, maintaining this constant stream of contact allows them to collaborate on every decision, which ensures they remain equal partners, always working in concert.

Their studio is in a giant redbrick building in a gritty sliver of South Brooklyn known as Gowanus. During the 1800s, this tiny neighborhood was a major hub of industry and manufacturing. So much so that the nearly two-mile-long Gowanus Canal—a narrow creek that slithers inland from New York Harbor, passes within shouting distance of their studio, and terminates just several blocks north—became so polluted with industrial runoff and sewage (and, allegedly, the corpses of Mafia victims) that in 2010 it was designated a Superfund site.

The canal's cleanup and renewal is slow and ongoing, but the massive, long-vacant industrial buildings that line it have over time found new life as loftlike apartments and creative spaces. JPL's building, at 543 Union Street, has the company name NATIONAL PACKING BOX FACTORY painted in massive white letters across the facade, a vestige of its former identity in the nineteenth century. Just above the final two words of the sign is JPL's corner studio, on the third floor. The space is a serene oasis of original details and minimalist furnishings. Welcoming, orderly, understatedly chic, and completely lacking in pretension, the layout and decor beautifully embody the firm's reputation for creating warm, textured interiors shaped by the lives that inhabit them.

The brick walls and exposed beamed ceilings are painted white (Benjamin Moore's White Dove to be exact, JPL's go-to white paint), and the antique pale floorboards left bare. The furniture is simple and streamlined. Set against the walls, each of the four desks—natural-wood tops on simple white metal frames—is paired with a utilitarian white rolling chair. Extending from the far wall into the center of the room is a white Parsons table set with four wicker-and-bentwood chairs. A sleek chrome-and-pony side chair, and another in chrome and black leather, are pushed against opposing walls, waiting to be called into service. A tall white-oak bookcase holds all manner of design books, both new and historical, neat stacks of *Architectural Digest* and *ELLE Decor*, an orderly array of tile samples, and just a few choice accessories—a pair of intriguing silver candleholders, an unusual glass paperweight, a mystifying metal object that could just as easily be a modernist sculpture or a piece of curtain hardware. On the floor, two big woven baskets brim with fabric swatches in every color. Six tall windows with plain white shades look out onto the street below, where horns honk and sirens scream, as if protesting the heat wave as well as the traffic. A lone globe-shaped glass terrarium is suspended from the ceiling with a length of rope.

The duo's individual wardrobes seem of a piece with their environment, striking that difficult balance between comfortable and professional—clothes that allow for whatever the day may hold, whether hoisting an armchair up a flight of stairs, or sitting down at a business meeting. Today Whitney is wearing fashionable high-waisted, wide-legged jeans, a beige T-shirt, flat brown leather open-toe sandals with gold-buckled straps across the top, and a simple gold cuff bracelet. Her round, brown-framed glasses accentuate her intellectual aspect. Amanda is in a cut-off denim miniskirt (most likely from Madewell, where her husband works as a designer), a white cotton blouse with puffed sleeves, and red patent-leather Rapetto ballet flats with low heels and small bows at the toes. Her clear-framed glasses are a pleasing contrast to her black hair, which she keeps in an immaculate straight bob that just grazes her shoulders.

Finally, Whitney's mystery conversation comes to a close. She sets down her phone.

"I had no choice," Whitney says gravely. She grew up in North Carolina and has just the slightest, most barely discernible twinge of a Southern accent, which gives this pronouncement an extra dimension of sobriety.

Amanda shakes her head in disbelief and silently tucks a strand of hair behind her ear. Her pale oval face is inscrutable. Somehow she seems to know exactly what just happened.

"No choice about what?" Neala calls out from across the room.

Whitney seems not to hear her. "How could I possibly say no?" she says to Amanda.

Amanda raises her eyebrows. "Are you kidding me?" she says, voice flat. She's from Michigan and doesn't seem to have any accent at all, but given that she's usually animated and upbeat, it's disarming to hear her speak with such calculated solemnity.

"*Kidding* you?" Whitney growls.

Amanda can't hold it in any longer—she breaks into a grin. "Of course you had no choice!" she cries out, laughing. "Of course!"

For a split second Whitney squints at Amanda, to make sure she's being sincere, before relief washes over her face. Then both of them are laughing. Then they are howling with laughter.

Along with being in the early stages of a decorating plan for this client's home library, they're also just finishing this same client's entertainment room, a big, airy space with a lot of windows. Early on in its design, when JPL suggested various draperies and shades, the client wanted to keep the windows bare. But the client has had a change of mind—hence the phone call. Now the client does want window treatments and wants to see fabric options before the meeting next week. So JPL has to generate a whole new batch of options to include in the package it's sending out at the end of tomorrow.

"We have to mail them fabric options by tomorrow!" Whitney spits out, doubling over with laughter.

"Fabric options!" Amanda howls.

Their laughter is saying many things at once: *There is no way we will have fabric options by tomorrow; if we don't have fabric options by tomorrow, we will lose this job; I can't believe our livelihood hinges on the fate of something as inconsequential as fabric options; really, is there anything more satisfying than thinking about fabric options??* It says something about how they feel about the job—and each other.

Then, fun over, they get down to work.

VIEWED FROM THE OUTSIDE, residential interior design can appear to be a glamorous profession, if not downright fantastical. What could be easier than sitting around thinking about paint colors and fabric patterns? In what universe could that possibly be considered a job? Moreover, only the wealthy can afford to hire other people to make over their homes; for those designers lucky enough to land the commissions, traipsing through mansions and country estates is just another day at work.

Meanwhile, an entire industry of glossy design magazines and home-makeover TV programs, not to mention perfectly curated Instagram and Pinterest accounts, is devoted to reproducing the results of this so-called labor, and turning practitioners of the trade into minor celebrities. Those of us who care about how our spaces look but can't afford an interior designer (me) press our noses against the windows to this parallel universe, hoping to steal an idea or two, or even to just escape, if only momentarily, the gross imperfections of our humdrum homes and their many compromises: the DIY kitchen-cabinet project we can never get around to finishing, the chic woven baskets bought to corral clutter that are now so jammed with junk they've become eyesores in their own right, even the IKEA sofa we're sitting on, which came upholstered in a shade of plum that seemed inspired at the time but now calls to mind rotting fruit. What is it like to live in a home without flaws, among original Eames chairs, hand-embroidered tapestries, custom-built kitchen banquettes, gold-leaf wallpapers, on and on? People actually get paid to make that all happen?

They do! But it hasn't always been this way. For centuries, interior design wasn't even a profession. For most of human civilization, well-appointed homes were the exclusive province of the very rich, who arranged their castles and estates according to whatever principles they'd inherited from their parents and ancestors. For the rest of us, living spaces were mostly functional, places to cook and sleep and come in from the cold. This focus on utility extended to furnishings, too: If you needed a new chair, you hired a carpenter, built one yourself, or just made do with whatever wooden crate was closest at hand. Certainly some people have always cared about how their homes looked and felt, but among the nonrich their avenues for expressing this interest were mostly limited to sweeping, scrubbing, sewing, embroidering, and making quilts. Likewise, since time immemorial every culture has venerated some objects over others and trafficked in sentimental touches, though these were by and large personal matters. Unlike the village square, the home was a private sphere.

Then came the early 1800s, and the industrial revolution, which birthed so many of the forces that shape our contemporary life, among them social mobility and a status anxiety that hadn't previously existed among ordinary people. Now that mass production and increased educational opportunities were creating ever more jobs, and factories were churning out ever more objects to buy, home decoration became a way for everyone—not only the very rich—to display their newly acquired wealth. But this was easier said than done. The rising middle and upper-middle classes, unwilling or unable to trust their own instincts, wanted—needed!—guidance.

So, toward the end of the 1800s, two brand-new, interrelated phenomena emerged, essentially in tandem: interior designers—that is, people who told others what to buy, and where to put it, who were hired by the rich; and home magazines (now known as shelter magazines), which disseminated tips and advice to those who couldn't afford to hire professionals.

Back then, at the beginning, the role of interior designer—or lady decorator, as it was known—was exclusively filled by wealthy society women who'd grown up among fine things and therefore knew how to tell others what to do with them. A century later, it's often assumed that this is still the case—that only people who were born into generational wealth, or those who married into money and therefore have ready access to rich clients, can work as interior designers. But that is no longer the case. Today, interior design is a thriving profession that's available to anyone who wants to pursue it. Some people enroll in college or graduate programs to learn the trade; others simply set out a shingle and make it up as they go along.

Jesse Parris-Lamb epitomizes this contemporary model of interior design professionals. Each partner was born into a working-class family far from the coasts, in what New Yorkers consider to be flyover country. Yet, each was blessed with that most elusive of qualities: having an eye. After a few false starts, each took advantage of the many educational opportunities to learn interior design. Now past the beginning stages of their careers, they are enjoying a measure of success and acclaim that promises more good things to come.

That is, if they can only solve this window-treatment conundrum.

2

Jesse Parris-Lamb is always juggling several different projects. When I first meet with Amanda and Whitney, in June 2019, they are in the midst of a more than yearlong residential commission in Greenwich, Connecticut, with plans to complete a major element of the project by the end of July. They are also about to embark on their first-ever show house, the Brooklyn Heights Designer Showhouse, which will open to the public in late September. (A show house is similar to but different from a standard residential commission, which I'll explain in detail further on.) Meanwhile, they are in the early stages of gut-renovating a two-bedroom, three-thousand-square-foot penthouse apartment in a historic cast-iron building in Manhattan's SoHo neighborhood, to be finished in February.

Interior design is a highly tactile, visual profession that involves a great deal of creativity. But it also requires a commensurate amount of organizational skill, social intelligence, and business know-how. The team's Connecticut project exemplifies the way nearly every interior design project unfolds strictly linearly (aside from the occasional hiccup), moving through at least nine core phases. To show what each phase involves, I'll use this project as an illustration.

FIRST, A BIT OF backstory on the Connecticut project. In November 2017, *domino* magazine ran an online feature called "This Home Has the Most Beautiful Sofa We've (Probably) Ever Seen." The article tells the story of what happened when Christian Rudder, cofounder of the dating site OkCupid, and his wife, Reshma Patel, founder of the fine-jewelry shop Quiet Storms, asked JPL to revamp the clean, modern three-story town house in the heart of Williamsburg, Brooklyn, that they share with their young daughter and their lovable pit bull, Ali.

As the photographs that run with the article show, the result is an exquisite bonanza of bold colors and patterns, clean-lined midcentury furniture, bright handwoven textiles, custom-pattern area rugs, and unexpected artistic flourishes, such as a lemon-grove mural by North Carolina artist Christopher Holt emblazoning the interior stairwell. Other highlights include a nine-and-a-half-foot sculptural paper lantern, also in the stairwell, and an intricate headboard hand-carved by a Moroccan fabricator based in San Francisco. The headboard not only looks beautiful but, because it's made from unfinished Atlas cedar, smells good as well. As JPL told *domino*, "The subtle scent it creates in the space is such an amazing way to unwind after a chaotic day on the streets of New York."

The sofa celebrated in the title of the article is a design classic, the Mah Jong, a low-slung modular seating system with French mattress detailing designed by Hans Hopfer in 1971 and produced ever since by the high-end French retailer Roche-Bobois. Usually the Mah Jong is upholstered in loud patterns and colors. For this project, to draw attention to the sofa's unique form and have the textiles complement rather than detract from it, JPL chose a palette of varying shades of red that, when the final product is arranged in a deep L in the corner of the family room, creates subtle tonal and textural shifts. Overhead, a projector attached to the ceiling allows the family to hang out and watch movies screened on the opposing wall.

The following month, December 2017, after seeing the

feature online, a woman named Serena Willis sent an email to JPL: "Hello! We have a custom built project that we are nearing completion on now in Greenwich, CT (we moved in about 3 months ago but still have some remaining work). In particular, we have a barn/entertainment space that is particularly challenging where we could really use some help!! Would love to discuss with you."

Amanda and Whitney emailed back immediately. They said they were definitely interested, but were booked for the next six months and wouldn't be able to take on more work until June 2018. Serena responded she was open to that timing, and they arranged a phone call for the following week.

1. PREDESIGN

THE PHONE CALL TOOK place on January 5, 2018, inaugurating the predesign phase of the project, which is essentially a research mission. Usually this stage includes a visit to the site, but because of JPL's workload a trip out of the city wasn't possible just then. During the call, Serena described in further detail what she was looking for, JPL asked lots of questions, and together they discussed the scope of the project and a timeline. JPL also explained how it charges for its work.

For decades, standard practice was for designers to buy furniture, fabric, etc., directly from the vendors, who sold solely "to the trade"—that is, only to professionals, and never to the general public. The designers would then add a 30 percent commission to each item in the bill to the client. This markup fee covered their labor, as well as their exclusive access to manufacturers and distributors. Most often, the bill was delivered as one lump sum once the project was completed.

Some designers still operate this way, but many don't, thanks to—what else?—the internet. In 2001, a luxury-real-estate agent named Michael Bruno launched an online marketplace called 1stdibs.com and invited several of his favorite dealers from Paris's legendary antiques market, Marché aux Puces, to sell their wares through his site. That first year, Bruno posted one hundred new items each week. Today the site includes thousands of dealers from all over the world and is known as the leading digital platform for the luxury market. One presumably unintended outcome of the success of 1stdibs.com has been a radical increase in accessibility and transparency across the design retail industry. For nearly two decades now, rare furniture has been easily available to anyone with the money to buy it, without designers acting as middlemen. Along the way, as manufacturers across the globe have established their own online stores, the practice of selling solely to the trade has become less common. In an age of Google and Amazon, clients can go online and look up nearly anything they want and get it at half the price.

Like many emerging designers, Whitney and Amanda have embraced a newer, transparent approach—they charge an hourly fee, with no furniture markup, and bill the client once a month. After telling this to Serena, they asked her for a ballpark budget: that is, how much she was hoping to pay for the finished product. By the end of the call, they'd agreed to set up an in-person meeting in several months to review the space—what they were now collectively referring to as the Entertainment Barn—and discuss the scope of the project in more depth.

Then, in March, Serena emailed again to ask if JPL could also take on the library and the living room. Over email, for the next few weeks, they clarified this new scope and created a new timeline.

Finally, on May 26, 2018, fully five months after the initial email, JPL made the job official by sending over their Design Services Agreement, to be signed and returned with a small retainer to be applied to the final invoice.

The Design Services Agreement lays out JPL's fee structure in close detail. After the initial retainer payment, the work that follows is charged according to a tiered system of three different hourly rates. The first and most expensive tier, the "principal rate," comes at the beginning of the project, when JPL is generating ideas about what the space will look like. The second tier, the "project manager draftsman rate," is charged during the execution phase. The third and lowest tier is the "junior designer admin rate," when the work is largely a matter of processing bills and contracts.

After issuing the Design Services Agreement, JPL scheduled a kickoff meeting for the following week to finally meet the client in person and see the spaces that they'd be working on.

On June 12, 2018, Amanda and Whitney drove to Greenwich, roughly an hour from Brooklyn.

When they pulled into the driveway, they turned to each other in astonishment. "We were like, 'Whoa. This is the biggest house we've ever seen! Play it cool, play it cool. Play like this is totally normal for us.'" They'd known the house had only been built a year before, but the classic colonial New England style was so well-done that it looked as if it had been there since the 1700s. The house is a stately three stories, a white-painted clapboard with dark green shutters, set back on a wide lawn on a long, quiet road. Two redbrick chimneys promise cozy winter evenings in front of the fireplace.

The clients are a married couple from New Orleans. Serena is a stay-at-home mother of four who used to work in advertising, and Quincy works in finance. Serena greeted Amanda and Whitney at the door and led them into the kitchen, where they immediately noticed six different types of coffee and espresso machines on the counter.

"Do you guys want some Dunkin' Donuts coffee?" Serena asked. Quincy was coming over from his office, a few blocks away, and picking some up en route, she explained. Perhaps they looked surprised. "Oh!" Serena laughed. "I own all these coffee makers, but I never make coffee at home. I just love Dunkin' Donuts."

"At that point, we knew this was going to work out perfectly fine," Amanda remembered, laughing.

Sure enough, the rapport was instant. The couple's three young children were running around, and at one point Serena left the room to pump breast milk for her infant. Amanda and her husband have a young daughter, and Whitney and her husband have a young son, and being able to chat about parenting helped break the ice. "It all felt so comfortable and familiar," they said.

Once Quincy arrived, bearing paper cups of coffee, they all sat down at the kitchen table and kicked off the meeting in earnest. Serena and Quincy explained that though their house looks like a classic Connecticut home from the outside, they didn't want the typical Connecticut aesthetic on the inside—which is to say, traditional and even sterile, with just "gray on gray on gray," as JPL puts it. The clients wanted something more urban and edgy, with lots of color. Serena in particular has a good eye, and a good feel for design. She'd thought she could decorate the entire house herself, but now she felt in over her head.

JPL was excited to learn that Serena had clear opinions and adventurous tastes. While some designers prefer not to have input from clients, JPL encourages its clientele to play an active role so they can help make their homes exactly the way they want them. Also welcome news was that Quincy was on board with Serena's vision—a refreshing change. Earlier, Whitney had told me that many of their male clients who work in finance, a field that isn't considered to be creative, tend to have consistent, conservative ideas of how they want their homes to look. For a lot of them, their design ideal is the Soho House, an exclusive members-only hotel and club that first opened in London in 1995 and now has twenty-seven locations around the world. Typically, the club's public seating and eating areas have something of a neo-men's-club vibe, with lots of deep tufted sofas in dark colors, leather chairs, and low lighting, in rooms with exposed beams and bare wood floors that lighten what could otherwise feel too heavy. To these men, this is what success looks and feels like, and they often want to replicate it in their homes. It's not that JPL doesn't like this look, but JPL knows from experience that it doesn't translate as well to a home as it does to a hotel. In response, they tend to push for a more humble luxury, something that is equally as impressive but more personal and livable day to day.

Eventually the clients led Amanda and Whitney to the Entertainment Barn, a modern, freestanding structure attached to the rear of the house by a glass-walled hallway filled with flowering plants. The barn is enormous—twelve hundred square feet, with a soaring twenty-four-foot vaulted ceiling. The south- and east-facing walls feature gigantic sliding-glass doors that open onto a vast backyard. A long black wooden bar runs along the west-facing wall, facing the center of the room; the north-facing wall holds a giant flat-screen TV. Amanda and Whitney could easily envision nearly anything taking place here, from a summer cocktail party with a couple hundred guests milling inside and out, to a seated dinner for thirty, to a quiet family night of snuggling in with a movie.

The Entertainment Barn sat empty, save for a pair of towering brass palm trees that the clients had already bought for the space. This element was a limitation for JPL—it meant having to work around these statement items, instead of starting from scratch. But it was also a useful indicator of what the client was going for in style. As Serena and Quincy explained, they wanted a tropical vibe. Elsewhere in the house they had used a lot of bold wallpapers—flamingos in one room, swimmers in another—and they were very much up for other such interesting approaches.

Next, Whitney and Amanda took initial measurements of the space. They work from architectural blueprints, but they also always double-check the measurements, just to be safe.

After that, they took a tour of the whole house, finally winding up in the library, which is two stories high and features a fireplace with a marble mantel and a spiral staircase leading to double-height shelves lining a catwalk. For this room, the clients had already chosen a ceiling light, a white pendant with a red-and-gold floral pattern. Again—an element that was both a limitation and a useful style indicator.

All told, the visit took about three hours.

2. PROGRAMMING

BACK IN BROOKLYN, JPL continued analyzing and synthesizing information. During their site visit, the clients had told JPL they planned to use the Entertainment Barn to host everything from fund-raisers and community board meetings to holiday feasts and birthday parties (the kids' and their own), and that they wanted a lot of seating arrangements throughout. Certainly the space was large enough for all that; the challenge was figuring out how to create multiple "furniture zones" that would accommodate so many different uses. "You have to do this dance of 'Is this seating arrangement close enough to that one so that two people can sit in separate spots but still talk to each other, but without being too close together?'" Amanda said.

While thinking through such functional and behavioral considerations, JPL also addresses preexisting conditions. In this case that meant the bar, which had already been installed and they'd therefore had no say in how it looked or where it was located. It was huge. They needed to make sure to leave enough space for walking around it.

External factors also had to be assessed, such as the windows behind the bar, and the room's several egresses—the one sliding-glass door that leads to an outdoor dining terrace, the other that leads to a swimming pool, and the entrance to the room from inside the house, via the glass-walled hallway. How would they create lots of different furniture zones while still keeping the paths to these egresses open? So they brainstormed, jotting down ideas and sketches as they went, until a cohesive idea began to take shape.

3. SCHEMATIC DESIGN

NEXT CAME THE CREATIVE part—drafting preliminary plans and considering furniture options, materials, paint colors, lighting, and tile. All the ramifications of the needs expressed in the programming stage are considered and reconsidered in this phase, from every angle. As Whitney put it, "We spend a great deal of our time thinking three or four steps ahead to what could possibly go wrong."

Like most interior designers, to sketch floor plans they use software called computer-aided design (CAD). Created at IBM in the mid-1960s, CAD revolutionized the engineering industry by rendering manual drafting virtually obsolete. Today CAD systems exist for all the major platforms (Windows, Linux, UNIX, and Mac OS X) and are standard tools in a variety of fields, including automotive, shipbuilding, and aerospace industries, industrial and architectural design, computer animation for special effects in movies, even the manufacturing of prosthetics. Whitney and Amanda first learned how to use CAD as graduate students and had honed their skills at their early jobs in design.

Because the Entertainment Barn is so big, to come up with a floor plan they looked at a lot of hospitality images. How was furniture arranged in hotel lobbies so it didn't look like a tiny island of furniture in a vast sea of carpeting? Particularly helpful were images of hotels in places such as the Caribbean and South America that integrate indoor and outdoor areas.

As they were drawing up the floor plans, JPL conducted visual research, spending a lot of time looking at and discussing options online and in magazines and books. The central question was, How do we riff on this tropical idea to make it layered, textured, and nuanced, and not just a bunch of in-your-face, on-the-nose pink flamingos?

Ultimately, they pulled together three different style directions showing various floor plans and sourced tons of furniture and fabric palettes that would plug into the different modules, all with a tropical vibe. The first scheme was inspired by the American West and the California desert. The second was a take on true tropical Miami. The third combined Southwestern and Mexican elements.

They also drew up what they call a "preliminary high-low itemized budget." Holding in mind how much Serena and Quincy hoped to spend, they'd found furniture options in a range of high and low prices, so that the clients could decide what they want to splurge on. Once all of those decisions are made, JPL facilitates the orders, then asks the clients to pay for them with a credit card or check. "We almost never front the money for the purchase of something," Amanda said.

All told, this brainstorming and design phase took three to four weeks, which is standard.

4. DESIGN DEVELOPMENT

ON JULY 24, 2018, JPL drove out to Greenwich again to present the client with its final design recommendations for the Entertainment Barn. This stage can be nerve-racking.

It's impossible to know how clients will respond to the design, particularly with something as personal as their home. In this case, JPL felt pretty good that they'd all be on the same page, but you never know.

One of JPL's many superpowers is organization, and Whitney and Amanda had come to the meeting exceedingly well prepared. They each carried a satchel of crisp black folders filled with inspiration images for the three distinct design plans, eleven-by-seventeen-inch drawings of multiple layouts, tear sheets for loads of furniture options, and quite a few fabric swatches, along with paint chips and samples of various woods and leathers (the "hard finishes").

The clients were immediately impressed. Serena kept saying to Quincy, "See! We were right to hire these two!"

Excellent! This really is going to be a great project! Whitney and Amanda thought to themselves.

Other designers have told JPL that it goes into these meetings with too many options, but JPL prefers this approach. Knowing what clients don't like is as helpful as knowing what they do like, and presenting more options makes it easier and quicker to get a feel for their taste. That way, the designer can tailor the next meeting knowing what the clients love.

As usual, JPL started by presenting the design plans and furniture layouts, then moved to the furniture itself, going with the biggest pieces first—here they pulled out the folder labeled SOFAS—and moving down the line according to size, from CHAIRS to SIDE TABLES to LAMPS. Next, they presented fabric schemes.

I'd assumed that a color palette was chosen at this point, but Amanda later explained to me that color palettes are rarely, if ever, set in stone at the start, but remain a work in progress, sometimes until the very end of the project. "Let's say a client chooses a direction—blues and purples—but they don't love everything we've suggested," she said. "So we go back and fill in the blanks, and oftentimes new colors get introduced. Then there's the matter of metal finishes, which add a different tone." Paint colors are saved until the very end because, unlike fabric schemes, they're easy to change.

Generally these meetings last about two to three hours—most clients peter out then after so much visual overload. But Serena and Quincy have a lot of stamina, so a full five hours elapsed—including a lunch break in the middle ("These clients always feed us," Whitney said fondly). It was exhausting, but also a lot of fun.

An overall style was arrived at that drew from all three

of the distinct design plans JPL had presented: a little bit American West and California desert, a little tropical Miami, and a touch of Southwestern and Mexican elements. A cohesive palette—whatever that wound up being—would make this mix feel harmonious and cohesive, rather than disjointed. A floor plan, materials, fabrics, and lighting had also been agreed on, and six armchair options had been whittled down to three.

Whitney and Amanda drove back to Brooklyn feeling pleased with how much they'd accomplished.

Over the days that followed, JPL drew up an itinerary for a furniture-sourcing trip in NYC with the clients, to review the furniture pieces they'd liked from the presentation and finalize selections. This is standard procedure for JPL, so the clients can see the items in person and test them out. JPL calls the showrooms to make sure they have the items on-site, and if so, JPL adds them to the itinerary. These scheduled appointments tend to start on the Upper East Side of Manhattan and wend their way down through the Flatiron and Tribeca neighborhoods, maybe concluding at a couple of vintage shops in SoHo. (When I asked if there was a reason for this method, Amanda paused, then laughed. "None at all! I mean, maybe just because that way we end up closer to Brooklyn, which is where we both live?") Whether JPL hires a car and driver, or the clients provide their own, depends on the clients.

On August 2, the clients came to the city in their Tesla SUV with their driver. Whitney, who'd never seen DeLorean-style car doors before—the kind that lift up from the center of the roof, like wings—had no idea how to get inside. For a moment she stood frozen, embarrassed. Sometimes working with clients who have so much money can present awkward moments, when it becomes blindingly clear that even though JPL is in charge of the design decisions, it's operating in a universe full of unfamiliarities. Fortunately in this case, Quincy simply showed her where to push the button, and Whitney's flicker of discomfort vanished.

This first trip was only three hours—enough to make it to several showrooms—because that's all the clients had time for that day. On August 14, the four took another trip, this one lasting five hours. At times the clients were attracted to furniture options that JPL hadn't recommended. JPL takes this calculated risk when bringing clients into the field. It's also where one of the many benefits of being a design duo comes into play. When a client starts to move too far from the original plan, Whitney and Amanda enact a subtle good-cop/bad-cop routine and gently guide the client back on track.

Finally, decisions made, JPL was ready to get the ball rolling.

5. CONTRACTS

Now that the design plans had been approved, JPL was able to draw up the paperwork required to obtain quotes from various vendors. This included requesting proposals for custom furniture. For instance, the samples for the pair of kidney-shaped custom sofas the clients had chosen were 140 inches long, but they wanted their sofas to be only 86 inches long, which required a total reengineering, given the curvilinear silhouette. In that case, the vendor created a drawing of the newly designed sofas. In another case, the clients had liked a vintage chair JPL had found, but didn't want to pay international shipping fees, so JPL made detailed drawings of the chair to give to a local workroom to make it. The furniture makers in turn produced new drawings showing how they'd pitch the seat, tweak the height of the arms, and narrow the width of the legs. As JPL works through these specifications, it also sets schedules for construction and materials.

6. BIDDING/TENDERING

AT THIS STAGE, IF a gut-renovation of the space is required—for instance, if a kitchen needs to be stripped of its old appliances, flooring, and tile—the designer may assist the clients in hiring a contractor to perform that work, then remain available to that person to answer questions and provide any additional documentation that the contractor might need. The designers also suggest vendors—painters, expert gold-leaf finishers, muralists, and so on. For the Connecticut project, which wasn't a gut-renovation, JPL only needed to hire a contractor to create custom shelves at the already-installed bar. So, in addition to pulling together furniture, drawings, and materials, JPL also sent out these small construction items for bidding.

7. CONTRACT ADMINISTRATION

ONCE THE CONTRACTS HAVE been awarded, the designer is responsible for defining the goals, coordinating the tasks and scheduling, and preparing for and monitoring construction and installation. In all of these tasks the designer must oversee quality control and performance, manage vendors, and liaise between the clients and contractors. The designer also maintains budget control and oversees all legal aspects of the contracts. It's a lot of work, more than most laypeople are aware of.

JPL embarked on the long, complicated ordering of the fabrics and furniture, and overseeing their completion and delivery. With most high-end residential commissions rare antiques are bought and custom elements commissioned from artisans here and abroad; rarely is a sofa or a dining table purchased straight from a retailer. Once the orders are placed, JPL checks in constantly with the vendors about their progress, as most of the pieces have long lead times. JPL tracks the orders and corresponds with vendors until the day that the project is installed.

This arduous process requires constant, day-to-day management of many different people in many different places, a great deal of organization and patience, and a fair measure of flexibility. As Whitney explained, whenever she works for the first time with a new vendor, she has to figure out which managerial approach will be most effective:

being a fire-breathing, draconian micromanager? A gentle and accommodating helpmeet? Something in between? In her words: "The back end is such an ass pain"—in this moment she sounds like the Southerner she is—"and it takes up fully eighty percent of our time. If you don't absolutely love the creative part, have a passion and talent for drawing and understanding how things are built, love colors and textiles, and always want to understand more, this profession then isn't worth it."

On August 28, 2018, the muralist arrived from North Carolina to visit the client's home and draw initial charcoal sketches for approval.

Things got dicey.

The muralist is an artist—he was happy to draw sketches, but he also wanted to leave room to improvise and couldn't 100 percent guarantee what the final result would look like. Serena wanted a clearly mapped-out plan and needed the mural done fairly quickly, in time for a party she was about to host. As she considered and rejected his sketches, she started to get nervous and lose patience—as well as lose trust in JPL. Jesse Parris-Lamb had to become a mediator between the client, who was new to them, and the muralist, an old friend with whom they'd worked many times.

To make things as efficient as possible, as well as to reduce tensions, Whitney and Amanda had to be there in person. They did a *lot* of driving back and forth between Brooklyn and Connecticut during this difficult spell.

"It was the hardest stretch of client interface we've ever done," Whitney told me. "It was really hard for us to figure out why Serena wasn't happy with how the mural was looking, and what she wanted instead. Because of that, it was really hard for us to figure out how to communicate with the artist, and even ascertain whether or not he could deliver what she needed."

Finally, Serena drew the line: "If I don't like what I see by the end of today, I think we should pay the muralist for his work, send him back to North Carolina, and just keep the walls blank."

Miraculously, by the end of the day she liked what she saw.

"We learned a lot from that experience," Amanda says. "Serena is a savvy client, but it can be hard for anyone to visualize what the final result of a mural is going to look like. Also, we were too accommodating with her pushing the timeline for the party. Ever since, we've slowed things down. We put *everything* on paper first."

On September 17, 2018, JPL met with Chapas Textiles, a

full-service handweaving studio in Brooklyn, to finalize the colors and weave for the pair of custom sofas.

On November 19, they met again with the clients to finalize barstool selection and fabrics.

In early February 2019, JPL met with a lighting designer to discuss lighting solutions for brightening up the bar area, and at the end of that month JPL met with the clients once again to review the lighting designer's plans.

On March 18, JPL gave another, final presentation, this one requested by the clients, who'd started to feel that the Entertainment Barn wasn't exciting enough and wanted to make the bar splashier. JPL made drawings of canopies over the bar, giving it a cabana look, and suggested alternative options for lighting and accessories. Ultimately the clients realized they did have enough going on in the room and didn't need to update the bar after all.

8. INSTALLATION

ON APRIL 30, 2019, JPL completed the first Install.

The Install is what it sounds like—the day (or days) that the furniture is delivered, the lights rigged, the room arranged.

"There was drama with that Install," said Whitney.

"Granted, there is always drama," added Amanda.

They'd ordered a set of six vintage barstools from Sweden and had them sent to their most trusted metalworking shop to be replated in polished brass. The day of the Install, they'd hired high-end, celebrity movers to pick up the stools and deliver them to the Entertainment Barn.

The movers hoisted and wrapped two of the stools, no problem, but when they hoisted the third stool, the seat lifted out of the base, and the base toppled onto the floor, getting dented and scratched.

It had cost the clients $20,000 to get those stools replated, and now, to make matters worse, everybody refused to claim ownership of the mishap. The movers pawned it off on the metalworkers, who pawned it off on the movers.

"Those are the phone calls that Amanda makes," said Whitney. "I just get too mad to be effective. But she's a bulldog. She calmly says over and over what is wrong, and that it must be resolved." Eventually, the movers relented and covered the repair costs.

Normally, elements such as draperies and shades would have been hung during this Install, but the clients had wanted to keep the windows bare.

When I first meet with JPL two months later, in late June, the firm was preparing for a second Install, scheduled to take place on July 1, 2019. JPL prefers to do only one Install, but oftentimes a second one is required because the clients want to rush to meet a party or holiday deadline before all of the pieces are in. In this case, the clients had planned for a party timed to the first Install, when the Entertainment Barn was only 95 percent finished. The second Install is for the wayward, refurbished stool, and the outdoor furniture.

9. PROJECT CONCLUSION

ON THE LAST DAY of the last Install, after every element of a project is in place, the designer takes a final walk-through with the clients to determine if any additional items need attention. The designer also discusses with the clients any care and maintenance of finishes, furnishings, and equipment.

10. ANCILLARY/ADDITIONAL SERVICES

WHEN THE PROJECT IS completed, the designer often arranges to have a professional photographer take photographs of it for the designer's portfolio. With luck, these photos might appear in a design magazine and attract more work for the designer.

WHICH BRINGS US BACK to where we left off in chapter 1, when I first visit JPL in late June 2019 and witness them confront the Window Treatment Conundrum.

They were readying for stages 7, 8, 9, and 10 of the Entertainment Barn. The project's completion date was scheduled for July 24, 2019. On July 25, photographer Nicole Franzen would travel to Connecticut to shoot the final project. Franzen is a widely in-demand freelance photographer who covers interiors, travel, and food for many of the top lifestyle magazines, including *Architectural Digest*, *domino*, and *Martha Stewart Living*. She is extremely difficult to book—JPL had to arrange the shoot six months in advance—meaning JPL had virtually no chance to reschedule the shoot day if anything went wrong.

Hence the office-wide anxiety spike that day in late June, when the clients called to say they'd changed their minds and want window treatments after all. There just weren't enough hours in the day, nor days in the week, to make it happen on time. JPL needed to scout fabric options, present them to the client, select the winner, commission their expert seamstress to custom-make the draperies, then have them installed by professional hangers by July 24. Usually a designer has at least six to eight weeks for all this. JPL only had four.

Yet JPL feels that it's part of its job to provide its clients with a flawless experience. "We are a luxury service," Whitney told me later. "If a client wants something, we do everything within our power, and then some, to make it happen."

And so, no matter what it took, on July 24 there would be window treatments.

No time to waste, Amanda brings a box devoted to the Entertainment Barn over to the Parsons table and begins to sort through its contents. By now, the color palette for the Entertainment Barn is a mix of wheat, burgundy, muted hunter green, various shades of dark brown, and gold. Whitney shuffles through a stack of folders on her desk and calls out to Neala to grab some more fabric swatches, and Neala walks over to the alcove where such things are stored. Armed with all the available information on-site, and a stack of sample books from fabric manufacturers, the three women start brainstorming options. By afternoon they know what they want, and Neala heads to the Decoration and Design Building in midtown Manhattan to secure fabric samples to send to the client the following day.

Founded in 1964, "the D&D," as it's referred to among those in the know, has long been a mecca for interior designers—as the *New York Times* put it in 1985, the building "sits rather unassumingly on Third Avenue, its riches hidden behind its gray facade like an heiress behind a limousine window." The D&D is like a mall, but it only sells to the trade—that is, everything is marketed and sold exclusively to professional interior designers, and never to the general consumer. Instead of busy "shops," it has serene, museum-like "showrooms"—spaces in which specialty high-end furniture manufacturers, fabric and wall-covering companies, and window treatment and lighting designers display and sell their wares. Back before the internet made high-end furnishings more accessible, there were at least 200 showrooms; these days there are 130, representing an entire spectrum of tastes and styles. The D&D hosts frequent cocktail parties, panel discussions, and networking open houses. As the legendary designer Albert Hadley told the *New York Times* in 1985, it is "the center of all our lives. Going there is both a delight and a trial—after a while, one's eyes have a tendency to start blurring after looking at so many options."

The next morning Neala arrives at work with a bag full of fabric swatches. She sets them on the Parsons table—a stack of soft squares in various shades of green, with a couple of burgundy options thrown in. All of them are solid, no prints, though the textures range from soft velvet to flat, matte silk. Most of the samples are from the venerable fabric company Holland & Sherry, founded in England in 1836, though several options are from the relatively newer—1928—Parisian fabric company Nobilis.

Then Neala pulls out the fabric selections that have already been chosen for the sofas, so they can regard all of the options in relation to one another.

After a great deal of deliberation, swiftly executed, the three women decide on seven fabric options to overnight to the clients.

3

More so than with most professions, familiarity with the history of residential interior design is fundamental to understanding how the job functions today. This is partly because the profession is so new. Across a relatively brief time—little more than a century—many aspects have changed and changed again, while others have remained fixed in stone. As a result, throughout a project the clients, contractors, and vendors can all have different assumptions about how the process should play out, requiring the designer, as the central point person, to understand where everyone is coming from in order to best navigate expectations and complete the task at hand.

One example of this is how an interior designer gets paid, which I discussed in chapter 2. Amanda and Whitney have been wise to develop a transparent billing system of an hourly rate with no commissions, in which they facilitate orders from vendors, but arrange for the clients to use their own credit cards (or checks) to buy the furniture, etc., themselves, directly. This method best suits the internet era. But some of the vendors JPL works with still operate by the old-school method in which only designers purchase the vendor's wares, meaning sometimes JPL has to front large amounts of money and arrange with the client for reimbursement. Not a big deal, but it can be stressful.

Further complicating matters is the unique position that the field holds in the world of work. Being an interior designer necessitates not only creative talent and practical skills, but also the emotional acuity of a great schoolteacher or therapist (after all, domestic spaces are loaded with personal memories and inchoate desires), as well as the social finesse of a maître d' at a hotel or fine-dining establishment who is well versed in the deceptively simple matter of social customs and manners. All industries develop their own codes of conduct, but because interior design is centered on individual homes—each a private domain operating by its own idiosyncratic codes—interior designers must exhibit an extra degree of decorum that can almost seem old-fashioned. As with the doctors and nurses of yesteryear who made house calls, decorum allows a designer to show respect for the client's way of doing things, while also maintaining a professional boundary even when emotions spike, as they invariably do given the charged nature of the space the designer is working in.

Knowing the (brief) history of the profession also enables one to better look ahead and predict new opportunities. Creatively, knowing at least the greatest hits of furniture styles, decor trends, and influential practitioners over time vastly improves one's own design work. If there's one complaint that every top designer I've interviewed shares, it's that the generation of designers coming up doesn't have any grasp of what's come before, and that this is detrimental for the careers of those starting out, and the industry as a whole.

BEFORE THE INDUSTRIAL REVOLUTION roared into the early 1800s, the average American not only didn't own a sofa, but had no idea what a sofa was (unless he or she worked as a domestic for a wealthy family). That changed quickly. The proliferation of new businesses and educational opportunities created a bottomless supply of jobs, enough to create and sustain a newly emerging middle class, while factories churned out a steady stream of objects on which this new demographic could spend their hard-earned money.

Between 1840 and 1860 alone, the home-decorating industry quadrupled, leaping from $7 million a year to $28 million. Whereas American consumers had once made do with
handmade, hand-me-down, or locally bought furnishings,
they were now overwhelmed with a previously unimagi-
nable cornucopia of affordable, ready-made, mass-produced
objects. As the market exploded, giddy euphoria—so many
wonderful things to buy!—gave way to bewildered indeci-
sion. Those who had never before heard of a sofa could open
up a Sears, Roebuck catalog and choose among twenty-
seven varieties. Where in the world to begin? How was one
supposed to choose which sofa to buy, never mind figure out
where to put it? (And why is it *still* so difficult?) For the first
time in history, Americans began to consider home furnishings an avenue of personal expression.

Among the many consequences of this paradigm shift
was the democratization of one loaded, woefully overused
term: *taste*. The concept originated in seventeenth-century
France, when the cult of haute cuisine elevated the tongue
from mere fleshy organ to delicate instrument of refinement.
Soon enough, use of the term had expanded beyond gastron-
omy, coming to mean the rarefied ability to judge whatever
was beautiful and proper in fashion, decorating, manners,

music, painting, theater, and so on. Only the wealthy had access to such realms. But during the nineteenth century, as the middle class grew, "taste" became available to everyone. It was the primary method of broadcasting to the world that one not only had money but was also refined, sophisticated, in the know—a step or two ahead of all those Philistines back home on the farm, who couldn't tell the difference between a crystal goblet and a jam jar. It wasn't enough to own nice dresses or a nice sofa; now one needed to own the *right* dress, the *right* sofa. Adding to the pressure, the machinery of capitalism doubled down on the concept of "new" and accelerated the pace of changing styles, so that one was never quite positive about what was in vogue and what was already considered passé.

By now, in the twenty-first century, the notion of taste has become so shopworn that it means several contradictory things at once: liking something a lot, the ability to make impartial aesthetic judgments, and knowing what is socially acceptable—which is to say, it means nothing at all. Today, having good taste amounts to knowing how to shop.

Far more relevant to home interiors is *having an eye*— by which I mean the unique and wholly instinctive ability to arrange colors, fabrics, and furniture into pleasing and harmonious combinations. Some of us have it, most of us don't. Like other ineffable qualities—charisma, genius, sex appeal—having an eye can't be pinned down or even learned and, as such, is generally admired, though never quite as well valued by the marketplace as more concrete and easily quantifiable skills. For instance, the architects who design and build the houses and buildings we inhabit tend to earn more money and cultural capital than interior designers do for making the rooms beautiful and functional.

Much has been written about the how the concept of taste filtered down from the upper classes, and for good reason. Equally as important, however, was the commoditization of having an eye. Indeed, the story of how this came to be is the most impactful, and underappreciated, period in American design history.

The story begins in the mid-1800s, with the collision of four otherwise unrelated forces: the Victorian era's surge of pattern and ornament (itself a mere by-product of the industrial revolution), the surge of mass-market magazines and newspapers, the induction of women into the workforce, and the birth of consumer anxiety. Taken together, they forged an entirely new role for women: the lady decorator.

Heretofore, design had been an exclusively male concern: male architects and cabinetmakers built and furnished houses soup to nuts. But as the division of labor was more strongly policed, and gender roles calcified, women became so strongly associated with the home that they were hardly allowed any influential roles outside it. Instead, they became sole proprietresses of the domestic sphere, overseeing how a house functioned and what it looked like. Rich society matrons especially spent a great deal of their time not only socializing and entertaining, but arranging their homes to appear welcoming, stylish, and above all impressive. (It's believed that the phrase *Keeping up with the Joneses* originated among neighbors of Edith Wharton's maternal family, who kept an impressive home indeed.)

As the nineteenth century barreled along, innovations in printing technologies had presses churning out books, magazines, and newspapers at an unprecedented rate, creating a bottomless demand for articles, news, information, and illustrations to fill the essentially limitless space. (Much in the way that the internet has demanded more "content" in this century.) Quickly, women with literary ambitions figured out that like their male peers they, too, could publish books—so long as they had to do with the home.

The first of this bunch, often credited as the "mother" of

interior design, was the textile designer Candace Wheeler. Born in the small town of Delhi, New York, in 1827, she possessed a strong artistic ability, which she used to channel her feminist impulses into helping other women become financially independent. In 1877 she founded the Society of Decorative Art, the first-ever association devoted to this burgeoning field, followed by, in 1878, the New York Exchange for Women's Work, where women sold products they could make at home, from gingerbread to doilies.

Wheeler didn't stop there. In 1879, she joined forces with the famous stained-glass designer Louis Comfort Tiffany to cofound Tiffany & Wheeler. This was among the first decorating firms in the country, and certainly the first with a woman in a founding role. Among their many notable commissions were the drawing room in railroad magnate Cornelius Vanderbilt II's Manhattan mansion, and the interior of Mark Twain's house in Hartford, Connecticut. In 1893, Wheeler published *Household Art*, the first of seven books she wrote and published about home decoration.

By now, the late 1800s, magazines about homemaking—cooking, cleaning, gardening—were hugely popular. Most of them were staffed by young women who, like Wheeler, had moved from small towns to big cities in search of independence and knew enough from their upbringings to write the necessary articles. In time, decorating tips were naturally included as well—but unlike cooking and cleaning, this rarefied skill wasn't something most working- and middle-class women knew much about. Instead, they commissioned advice columns from society women who, having grown up with finery, had the knowledge and the authority to instruct the rising bourgeoisie on how to handle finery themselves. By the late 1800s, these so-called lady decorators comprised a small but powerful cadre of populist-minded, entrepreneurial tastemakers who seized the pulpit of syndicated newspaper columns and how-to manuals to preach the gospel of home decor to an uninitiated public—the original Martha Stewarts, if you will.

In 1897, before becoming one of America's most important novelists, Edith Wharton published her first book, *The Decoration of Houses*, an architecture and interior-decorating manual that served as a bible of the field. (She never hired herself out as a decorator, however, instead reserving her talents to her own homes.) Other lady-decorator luminaries were the socialite Elsie de Wolfe, the gossip columnist/hostess Elsa Maxwell, and Dorothy Draper, known as the first-ever commercial interior decorator. Each of these women had a firm of her own and was a pioneer in exchanging her decorating skills and ideas for money. By distilling their creative abilities into practical advice, these well-heeled women single-handedly defined the way we regard—and even arrange—our homes today.

Take the contemporary living room, which is a direct descendant of the nineteenth-century parlor. Following the advice of her favorite decor column, or how-to book, the middle-class homemaker would furnish the parlor with her newly acquired sofa, along with a coffee table, one or two armchairs, and reading lamps. This arrangement became so standardized that it didn't occur to anyone to question it. Even now it's difficult to envision a living room that isn't some variation on that template.

The first documented use of the term *interior decoration* was in 1904, the same year that the first educational courses in the subject were introduced, at the New York School of Art (now Parsons School of Design). The field's first professional organization, the American Institute of Interior Decorators, formed in 1931, dropped the word *interior* in 1936, to become the American Institute of Decorators (AID).

The term *interior designer* became commonplace in the 1930s, after it was coined by the magazine *Interior Design and Decoration*. In 1957, the National Society for Interior Designers (NSID) formed as a splinter group of the New York chapter of the AID, which changed its name yet again, in 1961, to the American Institute of Interior Designers (still AID).

During the 1950s, gender roles morphed yet again. Gay men were flocking to a profession that was not only welcoming of their talents but also tolerant of their sexual orientation. Few of them lived out of the closet in public, but in the world of home decor they found a measure of freedom to be themselves that was lacking in the overwhelmingly masculine and heteronormative corporate world. In the 1980s, glossy magazines began to treat decorators like celebrities, and during this period many of the top, most name-brand interior designers were gay men.

Meanwhile, as interior design became a profession in its own right, schools devoted to teaching the necessary skills spread like wildfire. By 1970 there were so many such schools that the Foundation for Interior Design Education Research (FIDER) was formed to review and accredit interior design programs at both the undergraduate and graduate levels; today it's known as the Council for Interior Design Accreditation (CIDA). In 1974, the National

Council for Interior Design Qualification (NCIDQ) was created to develop and administer a national interior design qualification exam. (Note that becoming accredited isn't mandatory for working in the field; JPL, like most designers working in New York City, isn't accredited. Those who seek accreditation tend to live outside urban areas, where hiring interior designers is less common, and therefore practitioners are motivated to prove in any way possible that they are the most qualified and should win the job.)

The face of design changed yet again during and after the AIDS crisis. As with all the creative professions, the interior design industry was crippled by AIDS; it's been estimated that at the epidemic's height, one member of the design community died each week. Among the many devastating consequences was the inevitable loss of generational continuity, that invaluable passing along of knowledge and expertise from one age group to the next that unifies a field over time.

How DOES ANY OF this apply to the modern-day interior designer?

One lesson to be gleaned is that every influential interior designer from the past created ideas, looks, concepts, and approaches that are still in circulation today. Being informed about the history of design allows decorators to extend and build on these ideas, rather than merely "repeat" them obliviously, which amounts to copycatting and often looks and feels one-dimensional, like a personality-less layout in a chain furniture store. It also allows designers to speak in an extremely efficient insider shorthand with furniture makers and those who run the showrooms, who tend to be extremely well educated about the history of their chosen fields.

For instance, being able to tell a merchant that you're in the market for "a classic David Hicks–style wallpaper" is much swifter than saying something along the lines of "Do you have something with, like, lots of diamonds arranged in a grid pattern? Sort of geometric but not computer-y? Like, old-school classy, but with lots of mod, eye-popping colors?" (That is, David Hicks–style.)

Another important takeaway is that for however long Western civilization continues to mass-produce furniture, paint, wallpaper, fabrics, floor tiles—you name it—interior designers will be in demand. The US Bureau of Labor Statistics predicts that their numbers will grow 4 percent from 2018 to 2028. The states with the most interior designers are California, New York, Texas, Florida, and Illinois, with quite a few other states ranking high as well, including Colorado, Washington, Minnesota, and Michigan. As for pay, the mean annual wage is $59,120—meaning that in some areas, such as Florida, an interior designer can expect to pull in close to $40,000 a year, while those in Washington, DC, earn close to $80,000. Of course, hugely successful designers can make double and triple that amount, if not more.

Interior design is not a recession-proof profession—unlike doctors and lawyers, who are always in demand, interior designers can feel the pinch when the economy slumps. In 2009, at the official end of the Great Recession, the American Society of Interior Designers reported that 65 percent of its members were taking smaller projects than they once had. But when the economy swings back up, so, too, does the demand for commissions.

The third takeaway is that although more schools than ever are awarding degrees in interior design, pursuing a degree remains optional. In this way the field is similar now to what it was like back at the dawn of the twentieth century, when interior design was becoming its own profession, and practitioners such as Elsie de Wolfe didn't obtain degrees or receive accreditation—they simply applied what they'd learned from their mothers and grandmothers while grow-ing up in fine houses. Recall that the first courses in in-terior decoration weren't even offered until 1904. These days, though the majority of working designers do study the discipline either in college or graduate school, and many choose to get accredited, neither routes are required to enter the profession.

For those in search of more training, more than 360 accredited postsecondary colleges, universities, and inde-pendent institutes have programs in art and design. The overwhelming majority of those who attend design pro-grams find jobs upon graduation. The New York School of Interior Design, one of the oldest such institutions in the country (it was founded in Manhattan in 1916), which has been ranked in the top five of all such programs for the past five consecutive years by DesignIntelligence, boasts a 100 percent job-placement rate for both its undergraduate and graduate students. The other leading design programs in New York City—at the Pratt Institute, the Parsons School of Design, and Cooper Union—also earn high marks for ensuring that their graduates land jobs.

A final takeaway is that because today anyone can practice interior design—female or male, gay or straight, of any race or religion, and with or without a degree or accreditation—the only barrier to entry is living in an area without enough clients to support a business and not being able to relocate. One can decide to pursue interior design at any age or stage of life. In the case of Whitney and Amanda, both came to the profession after trying others first.

4

On a walk through the pastoral campus of the Pratt Institute, in Brooklyn, Amanda told me about the career she had as a professional ballet dancer—before she even began thinking about design.

It's a pleasant autumn afternoon, golden leaves skittering along the sidewalks, not a cloud in the sky. Pratt's twenty-five-acre campus in Brooklyn's historic Clinton Hill neighborhood looks like a fantasy of what an educational experience should be. Stately brick buildings—nineteenth-century Romanesque revival, Victorian, and neoclassical styles mixed in with contemporary designs—surround a tranquil, grassy quad that's shaded by trees. Founded in 1887, Pratt was one of the first schools in the country to admit students regardless of class, race, or gender, and to prepare them to enter the fields of design and engineering, while also getting a liberal arts education. That visionary DNA permeates the atmosphere today, most immediately in the quad itself, which is known as the Sculpture Park and features a revolving exhibit of more than seventy sculptures by well-known and emerging artists, faculty, and graduates.

As always, Amanda is dressed comfortably but fashionably, today in button-fly, high-waisted light-blue jeans, a white T-shirt with three-quarter-length puffed sleeves, and her red patent-leather Rapetto ballet flats. As she talks, it's hard not to think of those shoes as the last link to her previous life.

Amanda was born in 1980, in the tiny town of Richmond, Michigan, about fifty miles north of Detroit, where her parents had grown up, gone to high school, met, gotten married, and settled down. Her father worked in the automotive industry, and her mother stayed home to take care of their two daughters (Amanda and her identical twin sister) and occasionally worked waiting tables. Amanda's parents had never lived anywhere else or gone to college, and they wanted their children to experience more than Richmond had to offer. This meant a great deal of time was devoted to ferrying the twins to tennis, gymnastics, and ballet lessons in the surrounding towns.

By age thirteen, Amanda knew what she wanted to be: a ballet dancer. She practiced religiously, thriving on the rigor and discipline. At sixteen, she spent the summer dancing at the country's preeminent ballet institute, the School of

American Ballet, in New York City, and loved every minute of it. She longed to transfer there full-time, but her parents wanted her to finish traditional high school, and besides, they weren't thrilled with the idea of their daughter leaving home for New York City, of all places. In response, Amanda did some research and found the HARID Conservatory, a tuition-free professional training school for gifted young dancers in Boca Raton, Florida, that also offered a standard educational curriculum. She applied, was accepted, and moved there for her senior year of high school.

After graduating, she and her sister enrolled in Mercyhurst College, a tiny Catholic school in Erie, Pennsylvania, where her twin could play tennis and Amanda could continue ballet. But after only one year, Amanda was hired away by the Cleveland Ballet and quit school to become a professional dancer. (Her sister, meanwhile, transferred to Oberlin College.) In 2000, when the Cleveland Ballet moved to San Jose, California, Amanda did not follow along, choosing instead to study ballet at Indiana University's School of Music, with the idea that she could transition back to being a professional dancer later on. When she gradated from college in 2001, she was immediately hired to dance with the Cincinnati Ballet.

Amanda loved dancing with a company. But only three years later, when her contract ran out, it wasn't renewed. She was devastated. Looking back, she sees that she had slowly become disillusioned with the dance world and had stopped working as hard as she had before, but at the time she felt totally blindsided, with absolutely no idea what she was going to do instead. For more than a decade she'd devoted herself exclusively to ballet. To figure out her next step, she moved to Chicago to live with her sister. A close friend from Indiana University had transitioned from ballet to interior design, and Amanda thought it looked like fun, so while waiting tables, she also took a couple of classes—figure drawing, site surveys—at Harrington College of Design.

"There was no aha moment for me," Amanda confides. "I just enjoyed the classes and loved the process of learning something entirely new, how hard and challenging it was." She remembers being told to calculate the elevations and scale of a space with a tape measure and having absolutely no idea what that meant. "It made me really angry that I didn't know how to do it. And that anger made me really get into it." Eventually she solved the assignment, which felt great. In 2006, when her boyfriend, whom she'd met at Indiana University, and who worked in theater, announced that he wanted to move to New York City, she decided to go with him and apply to study interior design at Pratt.

Our walk has brought us to the doors of the Juliana Curran Terian Design Center, where Amanda spent most of her time from 2006 to 2009. When we go inside to look around, she's surprised by how much has changed since she graduated, a decade ago. The feel is the same—a spacious, airy hive of students engaged in various activities—but the room in which she took most of her classes has been converted into a fabrication studio. Back outside, we look for a place to sit down and continue our conversation, ultimately choosing an actual sculpture: a wood-slatted bench with a tall, wildly undulating back, by artist and Pratt professor Cathey Billian, called *Whispering Bench—Texting* (2014).

"I was so intimidated at first," Amanda remembers from her early days at Pratt. "They just start you right out of the gate, with an assignment that you have to stand up and present to the whole class in two days. I didn't really know how to draw, and the idea of presenting something without knowing how to do that really scared me. I thought I was going to flunk. I called my sister every day. I was so nervous that I was certain I was going to get kicked out of school."

That first presentation didn't go so well. But the second

was a lot better. The assignment was to find a building or some other architectural example and discuss its composition. "Or maybe that's the assignment I turned it into," Amanda says, laughing. She found photographs of an abandoned ballet school in Cuba and superimposed onto it shapes of dancers doing arabesques and pirouettes and other ballet moves in ways that mimicked the shape of the building.

"That's when I understood that design was going to work for me," she says. "I'd spent my life studying composition and proportion, but only ever with the human body, in front of a mirror. When I did this assignment, I saw that I could apply that type of bodily spatial awareness to designing homes."

Amanda loved the camaraderie of the school, and the conceptual deep thinking. It was exciting to apply the discipline she'd acquired through learning ballet to learning something new. Though she never mastered drawing, she did get better and better at giving presentations, and talking through her ideas.

UNLIKE AMANDA, WHITNEY HAD a hint of her future early on. She was born in 1981, in Waynesville, North Carolina, a small country town between the Great Smoky and Blue Ridge Mountains. In the 1970s, her mother had earned her associate's degree in interior design at Massey Junior College, in Atlanta, Georgia. Though she never pursued the profession—in part because Waynesville is so small that it didn't offer many clients—she did work for a while at the local Sherwin-Williams paint store, mixing paint and helping customers choose colors. Eventually she went back to school to study early-childhood education and spent the rest of her career teaching at a preschool. But her intuitive feel for home decor was evident in the home she created for her husband and two children.

"She made the house nice in such an impressive way," Whitney recalls admiringly. We are sitting at a table for two in a small, cozy Italian restaurant in the Prospect Heights neighborhood of Brooklyn, close to where she lives with her husband and young son. "She didn't have much money, and she didn't have much to work with. She was always taking hand-me-downs from friends and family, particularly her grandmother—my great-grandmother—who lived nearby and collected antiques. But still she pulled together a really lovely home, nicely scaled, tasteful, tidy."

When I ask how her mother pulled this off, Whitney

doesn't need to think before she says, "She took such care with her decisions and brought a great amount of intentionality to how things were cared for."

It took a while for Whitney to fully appreciate her mother's skills. But one particular moment made her see the power of what her mother could do. Their kitchen had saffron-yellow countertops, which her mother didn't like, but neither did she have enough money to replace them. Instead, she found a rusty-red wallpaper with dark green and blue elements that, when hung, completely transformed the space; as if by magic, the strong colors both muted the yellow countertops and harmonized with them, making what had been verging on ugly quite beautiful. "That's when I realized she was onto something," Whitney says.

Not much could be done with Whitney's childhood bedroom, which was furnished with a heavy, ornate set of Chippendale furniture handed down by her great-grandmother—a washstand, a dresser, and a big bed. "Too much for a little girl," Whitney says, laughing. So her parents let her pick out the room colors, and she chose a tan-and-salmon palette.

When it was time for college, Whitney briefly considered pursuing an interior design degree, but ultimately decided it was too specific and specialized for a nineteen-year-old. She wanted something more academic. So she studied art history at the University of North Carolina in Chapel Hill, graduating in 2003.

"I absolutely loved learning about different art periods and movements," Whitney says. "And in the end, it turned out to be an excellent foundation for what I do now."

After college, she taught art history to middle school students, until she and her boyfriend (they'd met her senior year of college) moved to New York City, in search of adventure. While he immediately landed an assistant job in his chosen field of publishing, it took Whitney longer to find work. "I thought I'd try working at an art gallery, but I was so naive about how people actually get hired. Just sending out my résumé was not an effective method."

Eventually, after scouring online listings for jobs, she found one that the qualifications she possessed were perfectly suited to: public educational programming at Staten Island's Snug Harbor Cultural Center & Botanical Garden. She enjoyed creating curricula and working with children and young people. But she was frustrated not to have the sense of passionate direction she saw in her boyfriend and many of their friends. Ironically, a panel she organized to expose students to careers in creative fields wound up changing her life. Among the Staten Island natives she'd invited to speak on the panel were a fashion designer and a graphic designer. "As I listened to them talk about their work, I was thinking to myself, 'WTF am I doing? I don't want to be teaching. I want to be an interior designer!'" So just like that, when she was twenty-four, she quit her job and went back to school.

A graduate degree in interior design is not required to enter the profession. But schools do provide training and job placement that can make the path forward a lot easier. It is a major financial commitment. At Pratt, for instance, for the academic year 2019–20, the first year of the three-year (24-credit) interior design/MFA program is $44,328 (not counting financial aid, which is available).

To make sure she really did have an aptitude for design and would be happy doing the work, Whitney investigated the New York School of Interior Design. Founded in 1916 on the Upper East Side of Manhattan, NYSID is a small private college that focuses exclusively on interior design, offering seven different certificate, undergraduate, and master's degree programs. Approximately six hundred students are enrolled. The average student age is thirty. And it's less expensive than Pratt. Through a combination of financial aid and scholarships, Whitney paid the tuition of $22,000 for a one-year program.

She also landed a work-study job helming the cash register in the school cafeteria, which helped with her expenses. She determined she absolutely does have an aptitude for design and definitely wanted to enter the profession. But the environment didn't feel like a good fit. "It was the first time I saw how rarefied, how snobby, the field can be," she says.

After looking around at the available options in New York City, she ultimately chose the Pratt Institute and, in 2006, started an intensive three-year program, only a week after her wedding. (A combination of federal financial aid, private loans, and scholarships paid for it.) She loved it immediately, all of it—her professors, her classes, and how interior design hits the sweet spot of being equal parts practical, rational, creative, and fun. "I am a supercompetitive person, and it felt so good to finally be doing something I was really good at," she says, laughing.

I'm about to ask how she channeled her competitive side growing up when Whitney suddenly asks me a question instead: "Do you know about Odyssey of the Mind?" When I shake my head no, she says, "Now, hear me out! This sounds completely unrelated, but I'm just now seeing that it has everything to do with what I do now!"

Launched in 1978, OM (as it's known) is an international creative problem-solving program for students that Whitney competed in growing up. Each year, a team of seven members works closely together—usually for the length of a school year—to solve a predetermined, long-term problem in one of five categories: Vehicle, Technical, Classics, Structure, and Performance. A strict Outside Assistance rule prohibits parents and coaches from doing anything but supervise for safety, meaning that all brainstorming, building, painting, sewing, and fixing are done by the team. Their work culminates in annual regional competitions, where each team has eight minutes to present their solution to the problem, after which they're given short-term problems that they must solve on-site. If they win, they progress to the State Finals, and if they win there, they go on to the World Finals, held each May.

"I've never realized it before, but doing OM has a lot in common with being an interior decorator," Whitney explains. "We had to work so closely together and really learn how to cooperate to get the job done. For the short-term problems, we had to juggle a lot of balls at once and answer questions on the fly. It was so scrappy and intense!"

I flash back to my first day visiting the office of JPL and feel I have a good idea of what she's talking about. It strikes me that both Whitney and Amanda have described themselves as disciplined, competitive people. How did they first meet? I ask.

Whitney pauses. "Amanda gets mad when I tell this story. But . . . our first semester we were taking a Colors and Materials class. Our professor assigned us to work on the same group project. I was upset about this. Somehow, I'd decided that Amanda wasn't serious enough—that's why she doesn't like this story! And, boy, was I wrong! Instead, working on that project together, I discovered that we share the same blue-collar work ethic. We're both from small, rural towns, and neither of us came from much. One of the many things I love about Amanda is that pound for pound she matches me in hard work, and putting in long hours. After that project we became best friends for the rest of school."

5

Attending school for a degree in interior design may be more common than ever before, but the long-standing apprentice system is still alive and well. The original lady decorators who turned having an eye into a bona fide profession first learned from their mothers out of necessity—there was no other way to do it. Once those pioneers professionalized the field, the women who came after them could apply to work in their studios and learn about design or attend one of the newly formed design programs, such as that at Pratt.

Bunny Williams, who is widely considered to be a reigning doyenne of contemporary residential design, did a little bit of both. She studied design, but she also committed herself to a long-term apprenticeship. Steeped in history, but responsive to the changing times, she practices both the "old" and "new" ways of interior design. At seventy-five, she is the sort of figure all the design publications want to feature. Her clients are enormously successful people in business and finance. She can't name names, but figured it was fine to mention her client Jack Welch, formerly the chairman and CEO of General Electric, since he's a very public person. (When I got home, I looked him up: a recent estimate of his net worth was $720 million.)

Over the years, I've been assigned interviews with Williams for various design magazines and newspapers, but only ever over the telephone. So when I asked her assistant if it was possible to interview her in person for this book, I was surprised and pleased that the answer was yes. The morning of our meeting, I took special care getting dressed and at the last minute added a tortoiseshell necklace—fake tortoiseshell—in the hopes that it would make me look more professional and worth her time.

In more ways than one, Williams serves as a bridge between the old school of interior design and the one that is currently evolving before our very eyes. She was born in 1944, in Charlottesville, Virginia—horse country, as she'll tell me when we meet; her father was head of the American Horse Shows Association. Her mother was an enthusiastic hostess and decorator. Williams's legal name is Bruce Boxley Blackwell; *Bunny* is, no surprise, a nickname.

Williams runs her business out of an enormous studio at the Fine Arts Building, on East Fifty-Ninth Street, several blocks east from Central Park. It's a pedigreed address, designwise. Built as a carriage house for Bloomingdale's in the early 1900s, the building was converted into showrooms in 1962 and now houses a combination of showrooms for high-end home-furnishings lines and studios for various architecture and design firms. These days, Williams has sixteen employees.

Williams has often told the story of her first design aha moment. At age fifteen, she and her parents went to stay at the Greenbrier, a luxury resort in the Allegheny Mountains of West Virginia that was famously redecorated and restored in the 1940s by the famous designer Dorothy Draper. By then, Draper was one of the leading designers in America, known for her trademark style of bold colors combined with classical influences. For two years she oversaw every element of the resort's renovation, and when the Greenbrier reopened in April 1948, it was the international social event of the season, attracting the likes of Bing Crosby and members of the Kennedy family. When Williams visited, in 1959, she'd never seen anything like it. The seed was planted. In 1962, when she turned eighteen, she enrolled at Garland Junior College, in Boston, Massachusetts, to study interior design.

Two years later, Williams moved to New York City to take a job cataloging furniture at a famous antiques gallery called Stair & Co., on Fifty-Seventh Street. Her big break came in 1967, when at age twenty-three she was hired as a secretary by the venerable decorating firm Parish-Hadley.

In this day and age, when interior design is practiced by so many people, it's difficult to convey the towering influence that Sister Parish and Albert Hadley wielded all through the 1960s, '70s, and '80s, the long reach of which stretches into the present day.

Sister Parish was a direct descendant of the first wave of lady decorators. Born into a wealthy family in New Jersey in 1910, she was rich in social and familial connections; her paternal grandfather was Edith Wharton's doctor and close friend, and Parish's first cousin was none other than Dorothy Draper herself. In 1933, age twenty-three, though she had no training in the field—she'd never read a single book about how to decorate a home nor served any kind of apprenticeship—Parish opened her own decorating business in Far Hills, New Jersey. In those early years she only decorated the homes of her many well-heeled friends, until in the 1950s Jacqueline Kennedy hired her to decorate the Georgetown house that her family lived in while John F. Kennedy was a senator. When Kennedy was elected president in 1960, Parish was hired to help redecorate the White House.

Overworked, she brought Albert Hadley on to help decorate the White House breakfast room. Ten years Parish's junior, Hadley was born in Tennessee and had apprenticed with the South's best-known decorator, A. Herbert Rodgers, before being drafted into the army in 1942. Five years later he moved to New York City, where, thanks to the GI Bill, he attended the Parsons School of Design. Two years after that, in 1962, he introduced himself to Parish. (Legend has it that she answered his knock at her door in stocking feet and a black wool dress and asked him to zip her up.) Eventually, she made him a full partner, and they worked together until her death in 1994, age eighty-four.

Parish is widely considered to be the progenitor of what came to be known as American country style—painted furniture, chintz, needlepoint pillows, white wicker, quilts, and baskets were just a few of the elements that defined her style. As *Architectural Digest* put it in 1999, "Her interiors as a rule were refreshingly unstudied, unself-conscious, and unstrained. . . . A Sister Parish room overflowed, to be sure—but buoyantly. It was romantic and whimsical but not sentimental; and, always, it was light. . . . Her rooms *lived*. They were friendly to the world."

As for Hadley, he made his mark distilling classic and contemporary styles into homes that vibrated with originality for some of the richest, most powerful families in America—among the more recognizable names are Astor, Rockefeller, Getty, Whitney, and Mellon. As heady as that client list might have been, Hadley was above all a practical-minded man. As he told *New York* magazine in a 2004 interview, "Glamour is part of it. But glamour is not the essence. Design is about discipline and reality, not about fantasy beyond reality." By the time he died in 2012, age ninety-one, he'd also mentored more than a few of the leading designers still at work today, including David Easton, Mariette Himes Gomez, and Thomas Jayne.

Bunny Williams spent twenty-two years working for Parish-Hadley, progressing from secretary to assistant to buyer, an incredible apprenticeship. Eventually she worked alongside Parish and Hadley as a designer. In 1988, she finally set out on her own, to launch Bunny Williams Inc., with three people, out of her guest room. Thirty-two years later, she's decorated countless homes, published six books, and launched her own home-furnishings line. She also speaks frequently on design, decorating, gardening, and entertaining.

OUR MEETING TOOK PLACE on a muggy Monday afternoon in early September. When Williams greeted me in the foyer, I was pleased to see that she was wearing a beautiful tortoiseshell necklace (real, or so I assume). She led me into her spacious, high-ceilinged office, and we sat at a big antique dining table. Williams exudes that all-too-rare aura of warm professionalism; it's easy to see her overseeing vast, complicated projects with grace and aplomb. As we talked, it also became clear that her bottomless curiosity has a great deal to do with her success. She knows seemingly everything there is to know about interior design, and this knowledge, combined with her innate willingness to try new things, means that her work is just as relevant now as it was two, three, and four decades ago.

When I asked her about the biggest differences she sees between the careers of those starting out today, and her own, she paused for a moment. "I have people come and work for me for two years, two and a half, and then they leave to start their own firm," she said finally. "Well, they've learned *something*, but not as much as they might have. I stayed at Parish-Hadley for twenty-two years. I certainly don't expect that people will stay here that long, at least not without becoming a partner or something like that. But the last ten years I was at Parish-Hadley I was doing my own work, and that's when I began to build my real confidence. There is confidence, and then there is *actual* confidence. The only way to achieve real, actual confidence is to produce something solid that you're genuinely proud of, and it takes time to learn how to do that."

Another virtue of a long apprenticeship is that you keep learning as you go. "The fact is, the more you know, the more successful your business will be," she said.

What would she advise a young designer just starting out? I asked.

"Get somewhere where you can learn a lot. You need to study furniture, and some design history. You don't have to do it at a university—in fact, half of the schools don't even teach the history of design—but you can educate yourself by going to work at an auction house, or a fabric house, or for an architect. A lot of interior design involves architecture.

In the family room of a Williamsburg townhouse, JPL arranged a classic Mah Jong sofa in an L-shape to create a snug corner for lounging, reading, and watching movies. (Nicole Franzen)

Upholstered in heavy-duty, contract grade fabric, the sofa stands up to all manner of toddler gymnastics (and party spills). (Nicole Franzen)

Floor cushions covered in handwoven textiles help the minimalist fireplace feel extra cozy. (Nicole Franzen)

A custom lemon-grove mural and Isamu Noguchi's nine-and-a-half-foot Akari sculptural lantern connect the third floor to the roof of the house. (Nicole Franzen)

Jesse Parris-Lamb (JPL) transformed a client's barn into a bright and airy multipurpose entertainment space. (Nicole Franzen)

A hand-painted mural establishes a tropical feel that's not too tropical. (Nicole Franzen)

One of the room's four separate seating arrangements (not counting the bar). (Nicole Franzen)

The ample sunlight glints off a pair of towering brass palm trees. (Nicole Franzen)

In this light-filled dining room, a woven-front sideboard echoes the sisal rug. (Nicole Franzen)

Rustic-chic leather seating is a JPL speciality. (Nicole Franzen)

Handpicked furnishings, cordoned into multifunctional spaces and united by a palette of black, rose, and chrome, make an open concept living space feel intimate and cohesive.(Nicole Franzen)

In this coastal vacation home, a low-slung built-in banquette covered in outdoor fabric (a JPL trick for high-traffic areas) gives pride of place to the greenhouse-style windows and copious trees beyond. (Nicole Franzen)

For the 2019 Brooklyn Heights Designer Show House, JPL began their kitchen remodel by ripping out the dark oak cabinetry and replacing it with a streamlined design in cream. (Kirsten Francis)

The geometric hand-painted "area rug" was inspired by an early 1900s sketch by textile artist Anni Albers. (Kirsten Francis)

Textured Spanish terra-cotta tiles cover the walls floor-to-ceiling, creating a rusty, rustic warmth. (Kirsten Francis)

Gentle curves—a custom bench, a vintage Osvaldo Borsani dining table with a round top and scalloped edges—mimic the wall's rounded footprint. (Kirsten Francis)

I'm looking at rooms all the time, thinking things like 'The moldings are too small' or 'That door is in the wrong place, I've got to fix that.'"

What are the main qualities that a good interior designer needs to possess? I asked.

"Foremost is having an eye. You're either born with it, or you're not. . . . One of the best ways to train your eye is to draw. Whether or not you're good at it, everyone should take a life-drawing class because it trains you to see scale and proportion. . . . You also need to have a tremendous amount of curiosity, and always look back: I don't mean in the sense that you want to repeat yourself, but that you want to learn from the masters. Most of the great artists studied under other great artists, after all. Studying great design will help you make your own design stunning."

Listening to her speak, I thought about how the internet had not only globalized the design industry and made design more accessible to more people, but had also created a lot of new wealth. I asked whether, because of that, she's seen any changes in her clientele.

"Back in the day, if my clients hadn't grown up in a pretty house, they'd have been exposed to one—maybe one of a friend of their parents' or of a friend of their own. They understood what a well-run, beautiful interior took, and what it was about. Now we have a lot of extremely successful wealthy people who did not grow up that way and have not had that exposure. Usually their only experience of luxury is staying in a fancy hotel. I've stayed in many luxurious hotels, but there are very few that I would want to live in."

I raised the matter of having strong interpersonal skills.

"Absolutely. I grew up in a big family, interacting all the time with older people, and that made me really comfortable talking with people of all kinds. Everybody has a different personality, of course, and you can tell in the first twenty minutes of a meeting whether or not you and a client will work well together."

Williams explained that different designers have different approaches. "I like to make people feel comfortable. I like to bring my clients along on the process. I hope they learn and that they have fun while they're doing it. I want their opinions, and I like to give them choices. It's their house, after all." But she knows that not everyone is like that. "There are plenty of designers who like to be intimidating and imperious—it's their way or the highway—and some clients prefer that. The clients who like that method of doing things probably aren't going to hire me."

I asked if she's ever refused to work with someone who approached her.

"Yes, absolutely. There has to be a sense of connection, and I know right away if I don't feel right about someone. Especially if they come in and say they've had four other decorators already. I absolutely am not going to be the fifth. But when it's a bad interview, both of you know it. They probably weren't going to hire me either."

Not long ago she turned down a client who wanted her to design his huge, three-floor office space in a big building in Mexico. When Williams went to visit the site, she decided it was too complicated and that she didn't want to take it on. She recommended he hire someone else. Four months later, he called and said, "I don't want somebody else. I've talked to some of these somebody elses, and I want you." Williams decided to do it. It was an enormous challenge: a totally raw space, not a single wall to be found, and lots of strange nooks and crannies because of the shape of the building.

How did it go? I asked.

"It was fabulous. I am so glad I wound up doing that. It was very much out of my comfort zone, but that's what creative challenges are—challenging! You get excited because you're not working on the same old thing again."

I remarked that she seems to love what she does.

"It's all fascinating to me!" she exclaimed. "The big picture, and then coming down to the small details, like how a chair should be upholstered. The details may be subtle, but they are so important. Inches matter.

"I love that I've never not wanted to come to work in my entire life. I love working with the clients. I love being creative. I particularly love working with the tradespeople, whether going to the upholstery workroom, or working with the painter on the job who's mixing the paint. I even love the business aspect. I don't have to type out purchase orders anymore, thank heavens, but I like thinking about the business, strategizing about where we are and where we should go."

I said that I couldn't imagine she had any intention to retire.

"I'm just going to keep on doing it until I don't want to anymore. I'll do it as long as I have clients that I really like working with. I met a new client just last week and thought to myself, 'I am really going to enjoy working with this person.'"

I asked if she had any parting words.

"Be sure that you have curiosity, and that you continually expose yourself to new things, and that you're hungry enough to be looking and learning all the time."

Before I left, she gave me a quick tour through the many rooms of her studio. Capacious, sun-filled, airy, all of them brimming with beautiful fabrics and intriguing objects, it was the sort of place I could very much see wanting to come to every morning.

As with many professions, internships have become popular in interior design—apprenticeships by another name, if you will.

Both Amanda and Whitney had internships all through graduate school. Amanda worked for Shamir Shah Design. Whitney landed an internship at Aero Studios, run by Thomas O'Brien, who had become something of a household name after the runaway success of his Vintage Modern collection for Target, which debuted in 2005. The five-hundred-piece line included bedding, towels, carpets, dishes, lighting, furniture, stationery, and holiday decor, effectively bringing his high-design spin on "warm modernism" to the masses, at affordable prices.

Like Whitney and Amanda, O'Brien didn't come to the

profession right away. Growing up in upstate New York, he assumed that, like his father and uncles before him, he would become a lawyer and go to work at IBM in his hometown. While a third-year prelaw student at Franklin & Marshall College in Pennsylvania, however, he took a printmaking class taught by an alumnus of Cooper Union, in New York City, and changed course. Just twelve credits shy of graduation, he transferred to Cooper Union to study photography, art, and design. "Everybody said, 'What are you doing?'" he told the school's alumni magazine three decades later. "But I was thrilled by the whole idea—for me it was about both coming to Cooper Union and coming to New York City."

After graduating from Cooper Union in 1986, O'Brien worked briefly as a graphic designer at *Details* magazine, and as an interior designer with Mario Buatta, who rose to fame in the 1980s as the "Prince of Chintz." Soon enough, O'Brien was hired away by Polo Ralph Lauren, where he worked on displays for the Polo flagship store on Madison Avenue, as well as sourced and bought furniture for Mr. Lauren's new house in Bedford, New York. In 1992, with items on loan from antique dealers and furniture from his own house, O'Brien opened his own firm, Aero.

Areo hired Whitney as a junior designer—this is the standard entry-level role and title, followed by intermediate designer, then senior designer, and then, at the larger firms, associate designer—when she graduated in 2009, but only part-time. She stayed there for ten months, then left for a full-time job as a junior designer at Roman and Williams. It was a stressful period. Roman and Williams was *the* hot design firm—among its clients are the Ace Hotel Group—and Whitney wanted nothing but to deliver, so she worked herself to the bone. She kept crazy hours, had trouble sleeping, dropped weight. After one and a half years there, she was hired back by Aero full-time, this time as an intermediate designer.

The experience was incredible. She stayed for nearly six years, going from intermediate designer to senior interior designer to studio staff director, developing flagship stores for Williams Sonoma and its West Elm, Pottery Barn, and PB Kids brands. This meant a lot of flying around the world on private jets. It was busy and stressful and hectic, for sure, but she learned a lot quickly. "As a boss, O'Brien doesn't care about hierarchies," Whitney said. His egalitarianism allows everyone to flourish.

At this job Whitney learned to use CAD and received a

thorough education in custom furniture and lighting. She didn't learn to source furniture and fabric, however.

MEANWHILE, SOURCING FURNITURE, FABRIC, and textiles was exactly what Amanda was learning to do at her first jobs out of school. It didn't seem nearly as exciting as what Whitney was up to, with the private jets and corporate clients. "We'd meet up for coffee sometimes, and she'd tell me all about what she was doing, and I'd think, 'Wow. She has really made it.'"

After graduation, the place where Amanda had been interning was hit hard by the recession, and not creating new positions. So she embarked on an old-school job hunt, looking up job postings online, and placing cold calls. She landed a job working for Bella Mancini Design, a small firm located in Union Square. She learned a lot about colors, and because the firm was so small, she dealt in person with clients a lot, which was a learning experience all its own. After three years at Bella Mancini Design, Amanda was hired as a senior interior designer at Eve Robinson Associates, a somewhat larger firm (of about twelve people) on the Upper West Side. She managed a wide range of custom-commissioned residential

projects. Let's say a client hired the firm to completely reno-
vate a six-bedroom apartment on the Upper West Side of
Manhattan. Amanda would create what's called a schematic
design of the space—for instance, showing what it would
look like to move the kitchen from the back to the front of
the apartment—and then, once a plan was chosen, oversee
the construction administration and decorative installation.
She also spent a lot of time drawing on CAD, a skill she'd
wanted to get better at. Though she did improve, even today
she doesn't think she ever got quite as good at it as Whitney
is—yet another instance of their strengths and weaknesses
being so well-balanced.

Finances were tight, though. Amanda and her boyfriend
had gotten married, then divorced, and at thirty she found
herself living alone in a Williamsburg studio with thousands
of dollars of student loan debt. "It was a rough period," she
said. Though she was being paid a salary with benefits, it
wasn't enough to cover rent and all her bills. To make ends
meet, she took freelance design jobs and did a little babysit-
ting. "I didn't buy anything. I never went out. I lived like a
monk, basically." Several years passed like this.

Little by little, she and Whitney started doing side projects together, on nights and weekends. "Now I was making

more money, but only because I was working like a dog," Amanda said.

Amanda soon fell in love again, remarried, and got pregnant. Around this time, Whitney left her job. When they landed a huge project to work on together, they decided it was time to take the plunge and found their own firm.

6

I t is July 24, 2019—the day of the Final Install for the Entertainment Barn in Connecticut, when all of the furniture and accessories are delivered and put into place and the window treatments are hung. Tomorrow the photographer will come to shoot the space, this phase of the project will be complete, and JPL will move on to decorating the client's library.

It's a beautiful morning, sunny and clear. All of the vendors are on schedule to make their deliveries.

At first, everything goes according to plan. That morning, like most mornings, Whitney and Amanda wake up at 6:30 a.m. in their respective Brooklyn apartments to help get their children dressed and off to school. Usually, once the children are gone, and the women are at home alone, they each enjoy a peaceful fifteen minutes or so in silence, finishing their coffee and thinking about the day ahead. Though they live in different neighborhoods, they are both close enough to the studio that they can easily take a quick subway ride to work or walk if the weather is nice, as it is today. But today they have to drive to Greenwich, to be at the residence in time for the first deliveries. So Amanda gets her car, fetches Whitney at her apartment, and they pick up their coffee to go.

The traffic isn't bad at all, and they make it to the house with plenty of time. From 9:00 a.m. on, delivery trucks bearing sofas, chairs, and tables arrive as scheduled. While the delivery people unpack the furniture, the contractor puts the finishing touches on the bar and screws the barstools into place. The lamps arrive. Check, check, check.

Finally, that afternoon, the window treatments arrive— the finishing touch. Against all odds, the fabricator had completed them on time.

Here, a plotline that had got off to a bumpy start skids into something closer to an avalanche.

While the drapery hanger readies his tools, Whitney and Amanda whip out their tape measures, just to be extra-sure. Five sets of draperies are for the sliding-glass doors, with three Roman shades for the square windows behind the bar. Once installed, the draperies will fall like water to the floor, pooling slightly at the bottom. The Roman shades are flat, meant to be pulled open or shut.

They work in silence.

Then: "Oh my God," says Whitney. She is holding a Roman shade.

Amanda looks up, remeasures the shade that Whitney has just measured.

"Oh my God," says Amanda.

The shades are too short. When pulled shut, they won't cover the windows.

Whitney is so furious she can hardly see straight. Amanda, who is also furious but slightly calmer, takes out her phone and calls the fabricator. Her hands shake.

Protests. Confusion. Nobody knows how this mix-up in measurements happened.

How it happened hardly matters now. Unless the fabricator agrees to fix the shades immediately, as in right now, JPL won't be able to finish the Install and go through with the scheduled photo shoot. But being able to fix the shades right now necessitates there being enough extra fabric on hand.

The rest of the Entertainment Barn is in place, and it is breathtaking to behold. Architecturally, the room is a classic barn—one giant rectangular room with a high A-frame ceiling and exposed beams. The decoration, however, is anything but classic. It is possibly the first-ever instance of a style that can best be described as . . . Tropical New England. East Coast Island Paradise. Yankee Shangri-la. In all my years of writing about design, I've never seen anything like it.

The first thing you notice is the sun, tumbling everywhere from two walls of giant sliding-glass doors. One wall opens onto an outdoor dining area; the other onto a lawn that dips down to a cobalt swimming pool. The ceiling and beams are painted darkest brown, like a coconut husk, and the wide walnut floorboards are totally bare, but polished smooth, establishing an organic ambience without going full-on rustic (read: no splinters). Throughout, a tactile mix of fabrics and materials—leather, wood, sheepskin, rattan—creates variety and texture, extending the natural feel. Then your eye catches a hawk in flight—that is, a hawk painted high above one of the sliding-glass doors, as part of the mural on all four walls. The background is white, and graced with just enough delicately painted flora and fauna— palm fronds, tree branches, pink flamingos, a green-and-yellow toucan—to enhance the tropical mood without overwhelming it. Real potted plants on the floor echo those on the walls.

As if by magic, JPL has created an indoor space that is

the closest you can get to being outside while still having four walls and a roof over your head. Of course, this isn't the result of magic, but rather nearly a year of painstaking thinking, scouting, scheming, and arranging.

A key to the room's success is the close attention JPL paid to proportion and scale. One might expect to see enormous pieces of furniture in such a large room, but instead everything is low-slung, streamlined, close to the ground. At center is a matching pair of slightly kidney-shaped custom sofas; custom-woven eggplant and gold-brown upholstery give them a cozy feel that takes the mod silhouette down a notch. The sofas flank a circular rattan-and-oak coffee table, and beside them sits a Mexican Bauhaus–inspired straw-colored woven-tule side chair with a black leather seat cushion. Three other seating areas are set around the room, each featuring a matching pair of chairs and a small table or three, all of it in leather and wood, with no two pairs matching one another.

But here's the thing: the room isn't merely gorgeous, it's also exceedingly livable. Like Goldilocks, I sampled each and every chair, and to a one they were supremely comfortable, the sort that, once you sit down, make you want to never stand back up. And though the room contains so many options for lounging around, there's also plenty of open floor space. It's possible do nearly anything in here: watch TV on one side of the room while someone else sits reading quietly on the other; run wild without knocking anything over (if you're eight years old); mingle comfortably with scores of other people, sipping cocktails and chatting and feeling fortunate indeed to be invited to such an elegant party.

Everything about the room broadcasts comfort, relaxation, pleasure—and the most subtle hint of glamour. Along one wall is a long black wooden bar, set with the five vintage brass stools with metallic gold woven through their upholstered backs. These metal moments, along with the brass-and-glass shelves behind the bar, and the midcentury brass pendant lights hanging from the ceiling, echo the gleam of the towering brass palm trees.

But what about the window treatments!?

A great sigh of relief gusts through the room: the fabricator tells Amanda just enough excess fabric is left over. The Roman shades will be remade tonight and hand-delivered in the morning, just before the photographer arrives. A close call, but also another example of how important it is to JPL to work with people the firm trusts. Mistakes are easily made, and often what matters is how they are fixed.

In anticipation of tomorrow, since the draperies for the sliding-glass doors, at least, are good to go, the drapery hanger gets to work. For the next several hours he climbs up and down a ladder, suspending the drapes from simple black rods. By the end of the day they are up, framing the giant sliding-glass doors. In the waning late-afternoon light, they shimmer like columns of liquid bronze.

RATHER THAN DRIVE HOME to Brooklyn, Whitney and Amanda stay in a hotel overnight. They are back at the house first thing the next morning to greet the fabricator, who arrives right on time and installs the Roman shades himself.

After he's finished and gone, Whitney and Amanda start preparing for the photo shoot. Like yesterday, the weather is gorgeous—sunny and clear.

Preparing a room for a photo shoot combines a little bit of actual decorating and a lot of make-believe. The goal isn't to simply document the space, but to show it at its absolute best, while also projecting an inviting atmosphere. All rooms appear much different in photographs than they do in real life, and talented photographers know how to make the best look even better. This includes working the angles just so, capturing the light to its fullest capacity, and "styling"—that is, arranging the pillows and blankets and plants and accessories so that they fall within the camera frame the exact right way. Ideally, a viewer will look at these photos, whether published in a magazine or just on JPL's website, and want to step inside, kick off her shoes, and stretch out on the sofa.

The photographer, Nicole Franzen, arrives at 10:00 a.m. on the nose and spends the next half hour working with her assistant to unload the equipment. There's a tripod, several fill lights, and a laptop on a stand, so she can assess each shot before she takes it, and then reassess it immediately afterward to see what, if anything, needs to be altered.

While the photographers work, Whitney and Amanda walk around the barn plumping throw cushions and arranging books and vases into pleasing vignettes. Their excitement is palpable, contagious. Motown plays over the sound system, adding to the festive and timeless feel of the space.

By the time Nicole is ready to start shooting, Whitney is arranging leaves in a vase on the bar. From across the room, Nicole frames the shot, and everyone converges around her laptop screen to scrutinize the image. The overall scope is just right: viewed from this slight distance, it's possible to capture the entire bar, as well as the area around and above it, showcasing the room's spaciousness. But the small details need work. First it's decided that too many leaves are in the vase. Whitney hurries over and removes two. Next it's agreed that the bar is too empty and spare, so she returns to set a pair of cocktail glasses beside the vase.

Nicole peers through the viewfinder. "No good," she says. "Next to that huge vase the glasses look impossibly small, like little shot glasses. And I think we need more color."

Whitney goes back, removes the cocktail glasses, and sets a green Tanqueray gin bottle next to the vase, worrying aloud that it's too big.

"How about adding that crystal ice bucket?" Amanda suggests.

Perhaps not unsurprisingly, it takes anywhere from thirty minutes to two hours to stage each shot. Later, back at her studio, Nicole will choose and touch up the best, ten of which will appear on JPL's website.

Somehow, once all three objects are together on the bar—the vase, the Tanqueray gin bottle, the ice bucket—the proportions click into place. Nicole shoots the photo, shoots several more versions for good measure, then moves the tripod two feet to the left, for a new shot.

It's decided a person should be in this next shot, to make the space seem more accessible and human. Whitney disappears behind the bar and reappears with a cutting board and a handful of limes. She pours tonic water into a cocktail glass and grabs the bottle of gin. Smiling, she throws back her head and pretends to glug. "This is a very difficult job!" She laughs.

A little later, the job does encounter a difficulty, but only briefly. While trying to photograph the pair of matching kidney-shaped sofas, they experience the rare misfortune of *too much* sunlight—the sun coming through the skylight washes out the pattern of the fabric. It's impossible to reach up there and block the light, so they have to hope for a stray cloud and then pounce while they can. Eventually Amanda spots an incoming cloud, everyone scrambles into position, and the photograph is successfully captured.

As they're setting up for the next shot, the client, Serena, appears, stylishly relaxed in a long marigold T-shirt dress with her hair pulled back into a low bun, and bare feet.

"What's your publishing plan?" She's referring to the shoot and its outcome. Will these photographs be published in a magazine?

"It depends on what you feel comfortable with," Whitney says.

It's Serena's home, after all. Whether a house is featured for publication is up to the client. Not all want their home laid out in full view for the judging eyes of strangers, even if the owners' names are never mentioned and nobody knows who they are. In this case, JPL is lucky: "Oh, I think you guys have to go for it!" Serena says, with real meaning.

Maybe it will happen. Maybe it won't. JPL can submit the photos to a magazine but has no say over whether they'll be published. Even so, that JPL immortalizes this beautiful space it's created for its own archives is important.

The afternoon unfurls, with Whitney and Amanda arranging and rearranging, making small tweaks, cracking jokes, and Nicole making what is already beautiful appear even more so. It's a workday, but to JPL it feels more like a reward for a job well done.

7

Interior designers have long maintained a symbiotic relationship with design magazines. Designers need their work published to gain exposure and new clients; the magazines need to publish designers' work to exist. If the Entertainment Barn appears in a design publication, whether print or online, odds are high that someone who sees and likes it will approach JPL to hire the firm—just as Serena had after she saw JPL's work in *domino*. Even if that doesn't happen, the exposure will enhance JPL's reputation, proving to other design writers and editors that JPL is a firm to be paid attention to. The bigger and better JPL's reputation becomes, the more likely its work will be published.

But the question of whether that happens is larger than JPL, extending to the present state of the design industry and its future. Though media has long been a dominant force in the design world, the rise of the internet, and especially social media, has so transformed the landscape that it's barely recognizable. An interior designer working as recently as the 1990s wouldn't believe how different the state of play has become. Over the last ten years alone the role that the internet plays in a designer's career has changed tremendously. For instance, if the Entertainment Barn doesn't make it into one of the big design magazines, it will appear on JPL's website and Instagram accounts and can attract potential customers that way. It's crucial to pay attention to these changes to best predict what will come next.

MAGAZINES FOCUSING ON HOME interiors—shelter magazines, in industry parlance—have long been a major engine of the magazine industry, providing a fascinating reflection of changing times at large, and the interior design profession itself.

The practice of featuring images of home interiors in books stretches back to eighteenth-century England. But interior design magazines as we know them didn't arise until the end of the nineteenth century, first with Germany's *Innendekoration*, in 1890, followed later that year by Vienna's *Das Interieur*. America climbed on board in 1896 with *House Beautiful*, which was soon followed by *House & Garden* in 1901 and *Architectural Digest* in 1920. This first wave of shelter magazines was intended to operate like fashion magazines, keeping readers abreast of trends and showing them how to arrange their homes.

In 1922, a new subcategory of shelter magazines launched with *Better Homes & Gardens*, which combined beauty with practicality. These took a page (or many pages) from the so-called Seven Sisters—among them *Ladies' Home Journal* (1883), *Good Housekeeping* (1885), and *Redbook* (1903)—a raft of preexisting women's "service" magazines that provided homemakers with tips and advice on keeping house. This new subcategory combined beautiful images of gorgeous homes with articles about the more humdrum domestic sciences. After World War II, when more women than ever before were running their homes without the help of servants, such educational content was especially valuable. Reading this helpful information alongside photographs of the homes of the rich and famous ratified the widespread postwar belief that keeping house was a woman's calling, duty, and greatest pleasure.

None of these magazines published articles about decorators and designers, however, who only ever worked their magic behind the scenes. A select few decorators, such as Elsie de Wolfe (aka Lady Mendl), made headlines—in her case as the first "lady" to appear on a Broadway stage, and the first woman to sue the US government over taxes—but the vast majority worked in relative obscurity, and usually only locally, acquiring new clients by word of mouth.

This all changed in the 1980s, when big was best, and luxury paramount. In response, the shelter category shifted from "moderate mass to extreme class," as the *New York Times* wrote in 1981, when Louis Oliver Gropp took over as editor of *House & Garden*, and high-end decor crowded out how-to tips on the magazine's pages. As if overnight, those designers who had long been darlings of the tiny, exclusive world of interiors—Billy Baldwin, David Hicks, Tony Duquette, Albert Hadley—started appearing in the pages of mass magazines, achieving celebrity. Mario Buatta, aka the Prince of Chintz, who'd grown up on Staten Island, became one of the most sought-after and influential interior decorators of the era.

As a result, interior designers were increasingly seen as commodities, with public profiles that far exceeded their ZIP codes. Though the famous names reliably dominated the shelter and design magazines, more content was always needed, which meant that even unknown designers, if their work was good enough, had a shot at the big time. Having your project published in a shelter magazine meant more exposure, and more exposure meant more clients, just as today. The relationship between interior designers and shelter-design magazines now became symbiotic, even inseparable.

The stock market crash of 1987 ushered in a new era. Glitz was out, humble was in, and how-to reemerged, most famously in the guise of *Martha Stewart Living*, in 1990. This time around, however, thanks to advances in photography, printing, and retouching, the homes depicted in these glossy magazines were exceptionally "aspirational"—magazine-speak for content that the reader wishes she could afford, but most likely never will.

By the early aughts, the shelter category was thriving, with several new titles launching in just as many years. In 2005, Condé Nast extended its wildly popular fashion "magalog" concept, embodied by *Lucky*—a mix between a catalog and a magazine, sort of like online shopping, but in print—with *domino*, a style-first shelter magazine that combined aspirational living spaces with DIY advice, arguably the best of both worlds. (Full disclosure: I worked as an editor at *domino*.) But even though the magazine won numerous awards and reached close to a million subscribers in only its third year, its success was no match for the rise of the internet and the 2008 global financial crisis, which spelled the end of not only *domino* but also other beloved shelter titles, such as *Cottage Living* and *Metropolitan Home*. (*Metropolitan Home* and *domino* have since been revived under different ownership, while *Cottage Living* continues to RIP.)

This was bad news for the publishers and editors of shelter magazines trafficking in high-end design, and the interior designers who hoped to be published in them. Consumers, however, now had plenty of other options for sating their appetite for looking at attractive living spaces, and learning how to replicate them. Since 1994, HGTV— Home & Garden Television—has brought reality home-improvement and real-estate programming to people across the globe; in 2016 the network surpassed CNN as the third most-watched cable channel in the United States, where it reaches 94 million households. In 2010, only a year after that initial wave of shelter titles was shuttered, Instagram was launched; as of May 2019, the app reached 1 billion users. We live in a visual world, and if any variety of content can thrive in this new era, it is photographs of beautiful living spaces—whether or not magazines survive along with them.

———

To LEARN MORE ABOUT the relationship between the rise of design professionals and the demise of design magazines, I spoke with Ingrid Abramovitch, executive editor of *ELLE Decor* and author of *Restoring a House in the City*, who's worked in magazines for twenty years. (Launched in 1989, *ELLE Decor* is still alive and kicking.)

"I still work for magazines, obviously, and I think they're crucial," Abramovitch told me. "But magazines used to be one of the only avenues for designers to get the word out, and now there are many, many more." Though that may seem to be good news for designers, and less so for magazine publishers, she thinks that magazines such as *ELLE Decor* still have a future: "Print is tactile, and design is a tactile subject. People still like to see design on the page. Besides, nothing is as powerful as having a major design magazine feature your story, in print or online. Nothing else has as much clout. The difference now is that respected publications aren't the *only* way to get exposure."

She called Instagram an absolute "game changer." For the first time in history, interior designers are able to show their work and make it accessible to the public without having to go through an intermediary. Aspiring designers can launch entire careers by just posting a few photos, even if it's only of their own house. But Instagram has also become an important space for select established designers as well, such as Bunny Williams. "She runs her own Instagram account," Abramovitch said. "She has such a modern spirit and is able to evolve. She's moving with the times. I love people like that."

The social aspect of social media has contributed to this transformation, by making it easier for editors to see more work than ever before, and to make more connections, more quickly. "Instagram is its own universe, where people are constantly 'meeting' each other, just randomly," Abramovitch said. "I might see somebody's work in the mentions of someone I know and respect, and suddenly I'm aware of what they're up to."

It's also easier for interior designers to reach out to editors directly. As has long been the case, many designers hire publicists to promote their work, but Abramovitch has observed that increasingly designers reach out to *ELLE Decor* on their own: "They cold email us. They DM us." She noted that because social media makes it easier for new designers to keep up with industry news, she's more likely to see and meet them at the design events and showroom openings that are an everyday fact of her job. Brands are also reaching out to work with young designers to create new product, so she becomes aware of and meets them that way, as well.

This accessibility begets a transparency that the industry has never before dealt with. The old way of billing clients a lump fee simply doesn't work as well in an era when information is so easy to find. "In an age of Amazon and Google, when everyone can see prices, clients are quick to second-guess a bill and worry about costs spiraling out of control," Abramovitch said. "The classic system of hiring a designer who goes to the D & D building to choose among products that are off-limits to everyone else needs to evolve. The modern consumer is not comfortable with that arrangement. An hourly design fee is something that people can understand."

All this online activity does have a distinct downside, however, beyond the basic crowding out of print magazines. "There's just not enough attention paid to history," Abramovitch said. "Let's say you want to be an artist or an art collector. If you walk into an art gallery, or a museum, and you've never heard of Picasso or Matisse or Alice Neel, how can you even see what you're looking at? It gives you a richer understanding of art if you know the precedents. The same goes for interior design. In order to be a great designer, you need to know the designers who came before you, and you also need an understanding of architecture and the social history of how people have lived."

When I asked if she had any advice for aspiring designers, she paused for a moment, then said, "Don't be afraid to promote yourself. There is so much noise these days that you have to work to get noticed."

WHEN IT COMES TO the necessity for self-promotion, Meghan Healy's design career could be considered a cautionary tale.

Now in her midforties, Healy wears her straight brown hair in a short pixie cut and speaks matter-of-factly, direct and to the point. Her path to the design world was circuitous. Born in Los Angeles, California, she took early to dance and enjoyed a career in musical theater that brought her from California to New York and on to Europe. When she tired of dancing, she found success in New York as an account manager at a major advertising firm, helping to shepherd global accounts such as IBM and AT&T. Here she also met a copywriter who soon became her husband.

Eventually, her husband decided to leave advertising and go back to school for creative writing. After he finished his MFA program and was offered a short-term teaching job in San Francisco, Healy's company transferred her to an office there. One afternoon, driving along the Pacific Coast Highway, her husband turned to her and asked, "What's next for you?"

"Out of nowhere, I said that I'd always wanted to go back to school for interior design," she said, surprising even herself. "I didn't know that's how I felt until the words came out of my mouth. But I was tired of the corporate world, and I'd always loved fabrics, texture, and color. He'd made a huge leap—why shouldn't I?"

With great excitement, in 2004 she enrolled in an eighteen-month program at San Francisco's Fashion Institute of Design & Merchandising (FIDM). She was also terrified. She was twenty-nine. In high school and college she'd been an inconsistent student, throwing everything she had into a dance performance or theater production and ignoring the rest of her studies. She worried that she'd continue those patterns now, as an adult. Instead, the opposite occurred. She loved being in school, and she did well. Thanks to her careers in musical theater and advertising, she was practiced at standing up and giving presentations. Being older than most of her peers, she also connected with her teachers more easily.

Healy finished the program at the end of 2005 and was immediately hired as an assistant designer for the Wiseman Group, a midsize high-end residential-interiors firm that's among the most esteemed in the San Francisco Bay Area. While in school, she'd learned the fundamental elements of interior design; here, she learned how to start a project and see it through to the end with complete thoroughness, never cutting corners, indeed being quite formal about it. She stayed for six years.

"It was an amazing experience," Healy remembers. "Paul Wiseman has such a generous spirit, both as an employer and as a designer. He has an almost childlike enthusiasm and passion for design, but also for history and art and everything that led up to the moment that was the reference point for whatever project we were working on. He was an incredible person to work with. All confidence, no ego. Very sure of himself, but without the need to trample on anyone else's spirit. And he could not have cared less where a good idea came from—he just wanted the idea. As a result, everyone worked their asses off for him, not because they were afraid, but because he was so wonderful."

When Healy started the job, about fifty people were on staff. She fell headlong in love with the creative process, from talking with clients to discover what they wanted and needed, to researching architectural periods. She often traveled with clients. If a home was inspired by a particular Italian style, for instance, they'd go to Italy to look at the original sources of that design. Healy loved being able to shop for fabrics, wandering through showrooms and touching everything she saw, squishing it through her fingers, trying it on in her mind: How would this linen feel to nap on? To sit on while wearing shorts? Once, she was handed a client's favorite dress and asked to create a design from the trim, which was then turned into a custom embroidery trim for curtains. "It was so fun, so creative," she said.

Then, in 2011, her husband, who had returned to advertising, was offered a big job in Los Angeles that he couldn't refuse, and the family relocated (by now they had a young son). A recruiter placed Healy with a high-end firm, but she could immediately see that the environment was not what she was used to, and not anywhere near what she wanted. It was rigidly hierarchical, and tense—everyone there struck her as unhappy. She stayed one day.

After that brief flirtation, she completed a few one-off projects for high-end clients, as a freelancer, but she didn't like it. Doing all of the necessary paperwork on her own, without the help of an accounting department, was overwhelmingly onerous.

"When you're on your own, without the support of a big firm, the creative part of the job is only twenty percent of it," she said. "The rest is project management, budgets, resale certificates, sales tax, orders, technical drawings, follow-ups."

Healy decided to switch tracks altogether and set up her own consulting business for "normal middle-class people." That is, clients who couldn't afford a full-service designer and didn't want one anyhow; all they needed was some direction and help buying furniture and setting up their homes. She created a website and presented herself as an experienced design professional for hire, who on the strength of a two-hour consultation could help you figure out your living space. What could go wrong?

A lot, it turns out.

Plenty of people seemed willing to pay for such a service. But getting her name out there so those potential clients knew she existed would require an enormous amount of marketing and promotion, none of which she was remotely interested in devoting time to.

"I learned a lot about myself," she said. "Namely, that I'm a terrible entrepreneur. I hate social media. I never charge enough, and I give away too much of my time. It took starting my own business for me to discover that I suck at the business side of it all, and that I am much happier working for someone else. I could have made four times what I was making, but my business model was such that I simply couldn't make a living." She kept at it for four years—"but only in a half-assed way. It was just absolutely the wrong choice for me."

When her son reached fifth grade and was self-sufficient in such matters as making his lunch, she gave up design altogether and moved on. Today she has a job she loves, working—for someone else—in educational technology.

Mikel Welch might be the polar opposite of Meghan Healy. For one, he happily runs his own residential interior design business in New York City. So happily that he often appears as a TV personality, most recently as the newest cast member of TLC's hugely popular reality decorating show, *Trading Spaces*. With his dapper, old-school style—a typical Welch look is a button-down shirt, bow tie, vest, and pocket watch—and bright, welcoming smile, he is a natural for the screen. He wouldn't have achieved any of this without his innate knack for self-promotion (along with great talent, a tolerance for risk, and an outstanding work ethic). He launched his career in the unlikeliest of places: Craigslist. The bare-bones classified advertisements website that launched in San Francisco in 1995, expanded across the United States in 2000, and now covers seventy countries couldn't seem further removed from the world of high-end residential design. If anywhere on the internet could use a makeover, Craigslist is it. But when Welch was starting out, back before Instagram and even Facebook, Craiglist provided the easiest way to connect to a wide audience.

Welch was born in 1979 in Southfield, Michigan, a suburb of Detroit. After high school, he enrolled in Morehouse College, a private, historically black men's school in Atlanta, Georgia, graduating in 2002 with a BA in business administration. "After that, I didn't know *what* to do," he told me over the telephone. "When I spoke with my mother about it, she told me I needed to find my passion, and that I'd find it by discovering whatever I was willing to do for free. At the time, that didn't make any sense to me. I was in my early twenties. I wanted to pay my bills, pay off my student loans. So I thought, 'Okay, well, I like clothes. I'll go get a job at Bloomingdale's and figure it out.'"

He had his aha moment one afternoon at work. After he spent thirty-five minutes of his forty-minute break idly browsing through Crate & Barrel, something clicked. He thought about all the design magazines he had stacked up in his apartment. All the home accessories he'd bought at Target. In short order, he left Bloomingdale's to work at Storehouse Furniture, an early leader in selling well-designed, well-priced contemporary furnishings. Quickly he was promoted from salesperson to buyer in the corporate office. "I was in charge of, say, sending a bunch of coffee tables to *Architectural Digest* for a roundup of the best ones on the market. Or sending a bunch of stuff to Nate Berkus, so he could talk about it on *Oprah*. I was annoyed. I was responsible for shipping furniture when what I really wanted was to be designing."

One slow morning, sipping coffee and scrolling through Craigslist, he saw a posting for a design assistant. He applied, got the job. "It was just the two of us, so I learned how to do everything. I learned the art of how to conduct consultations with clients. I learned the business aspect, the building, the booking, the sourcing for furniture. And I learned that I was talented enough to do the design portion on my own."

After working for the designer for about a year, Welch returned to Craigslist, this time not to look for a new job, but to offer up his own services—pro bono. That is, as he described it in his ad, he'd design a room for free so long as the client paid for the furniture. "That was my 'promotion.'" He laughed. "That's how I built my portfolio. One free room at a time."

Portfolio in hand, he decided to leave Atlanta and take his one-man show on the road. Once again he returned to Craigslist, posting the same ad for free work, but this time on the pages for Miami, Los Angeles, and New York. He figured he'd move to whichever city gave him the most hits. The very next day, he received an email from the online publisher WebMD. They needed someone to design a rooftop launch party. "It was event planning, not design, but it was my cue," he said. In short order he applied online for a job at the Container Store in Manhattan, illegally sublet his apartment, and moved to New York.

"At the Container Store, my life changed," he said. "I worked from eight p.m. to two a.m. unloading boxes of materials from a truck. One night I ran into a woman who'd heard that I wanted to work in interior design. She asked me to come assist her on a project. Basically, she was prop styling for a high-society woman who did interior design as a hobby. In a way, we were her ghost designers, assisting her with residential projects and designer show houses."

Where once he worked with a $5,000 budget for an entire apartment, now he was working with a $250,000 budget for a single room. He kept building his portfolio.

"From there, I got kind of cocky, to be honest. I was still building my portfolio by posting my free ad on Craigslist, and I got a call from a real estate developer who needed someone to do several model-home units." Welch left his job at the Container Store and threw himself into the new work. Then: "One of them didn't come out as nicely as I'd wanted, and I was let go."

Now he was out of work altogether, so he went back to retail, this time at the furniture store CB2. He stayed for two years. One morning, a man in his sixties dashed into the store with a group of twenty-somethings. They ran all over the place, grabbing lamps and pillows and trays and bringing them to the register. "I was like, 'What in the world is this grown man doing with all these young people? What is up with all this stuff they're buying?' I had to find out."

The man explained that he was a set decorator for the Showtime program *Dexter*. The show was based in LA, but a scene was being shot in New York. He gave Welch his number and said that if he ever came to LA, he'd give him work.

That was all the prompting Welch needed. That afternoon he asked his boss to transfer him to the LA store, and within the week he was flying across the country, ready to start a new chapter.

Welch called the *Dexter* guy. He didn't pick up. Welch called again. No answer. *All right*, Welch decided, *I'm in LA now, so I might as well figure out how to make it work.*

He vowed that if anyone ever came into the store again in the same manner, dashing around and tossing stuff on the counter, he would ask if he could shadow the person for a day, for free. "I knew that if someone would just let me get in the door that I could open up other doors."

His first week on the job, he pulled off exactly that and wound up picking up furniture and hauling it to sets for the HGTV star Emily Henderson. After a month of working for free, he was glad to have his foot in the door, but he still needed money, so he took the bold move of flat-out lying on his résumé, updating it to say that he'd been art director of the show for a full season. A week later he got a call from the Style Network, was interviewed to be art director on a show, and got the job on-site.

"I very quickly had to figure a lot of things out. When you're self-taught, you run into certain, ah, hiccups," he said wryly. "Certain skill sets. I didn't know how to make renderings on CAD, for instance. But I could sketch out a stick drawing and explain what I wanted to do. The solution was to pair me with a young woman who knew how to do renderings."

Welch stayed with that job for a year. In 2011, a coworker told him about a reality show for HGTV called *Design Star*. Welch was among two thousand people to audition—and one of only two who were selected. The rest is history. Since then, he's worked as a set decorator and on-air designer for comedian Steve Harvey's talk show, where he met the likes of Michelle Obama and Halle Barry, designed sets for the network TV shows *I Love Kellie Pickler* and *Real Housewives of Atlanta*, designed Nick Jonas's tour bus, and done quite a few show houses. Oh, yes, along the way he also grew and maintained his own design business. And joined the cast of

Trading Spaces. And hired a publicist and a manager to help him keep it all in motion.

"My life is crazy like that," he said, laughing. "And that's just the short version. It's been really hard—I've left a lot out. A lot of sleeping on people's sofas, a little living on food stamps."

I asked if he ever wishes he'd gone to design school.

"At times, yes. Was it harder to do it this way? Definitely. But I've been free to take risks. And the rewards have been bigger. I get a lot of respect from people for my story, and if I did it differently, this story wouldn't be mine. If I had to do it all over again, I'd do it the exact same way."

The historical roster of iconic interior designers, from Elsie de Wolfe to Albert Hadley, is predominantly white, and even today nonwhite designers don't get as much representation. "It's tougher for the black community," Welch said. "There's definitely an audience there, but black designers don't get enough press. Lack of diversity and inclusion is a big problem. Another is a lack of understanding how the design world works. A lot of people have the misconception that when you do great work, the magazine editors and potential clients will come calling. But a lot of the press I get is because I pay a publicist. It's important that people know that, whether they're already established or just starting out."

Any other advice for those entering the profession? "Reach out to someone and get a mentor. So many young people try to do things on their own. But when you have a mentor, you learn on their dime, and you learn from their mistakes. Most important, you *learn*. The world is changing now. There's a stigma around working for no pay. But in my experience the biggest jobs I've gotten were because I asked someone if I could do it for free."

8

At last, it's September 26, 2019, the opening of JPL's Brooklyn Heights Designer Showhouse. JPL has been working steadily toward this event since early June. The evening is overcast, the narrow streets nearly empty, the sky overhead a muted gray. But when I turn the corner, the gentle, hushed atmosphere crackles to life. A line of people are waiting to walk through the front door of 13 Pineapple Street. (Yes, even the street names are charming here.)

Among New Yorkers, Brooklyn Heights is often considered the most beautiful neighborhood in all the borough, a quiet, affluent enclave of historic brownstones, many built before the Civil War, sheltered by tall, leafy trees, all within a short walk to the East River. It's no wonder that more than a few feature films and television shows have been shot here, from the Cher vehicle *Moonstruck* to Martin Scorsese's film adaptation of Edith Wharton's classic novel *The Age of Innocence*; even Scorsese's own classic *Taxi Driver* features a climactic scene here.

In the 1940s, when New York City's controversial master builder Robert Moses proposed routing the Brooklyn–Queens Expressway straight through the middle of Brooklyn Heights, a group known as the Brooklyn Heights Association (BHA) fought for the highway to be moved to the perimeter of the neighborhood, alongside the river. So it came to pass. As if to reward this ingenious solution, the New York City Department of Transportation built on top of the new stretch of highway a nearly two-thousand-foot-long pedestrian walkway with breathtaking views of Lower Manhattan and the New York Harbor. Today known as the world-famous Brooklyn Heights Promenade, it is alive every night of the year with families taking after-dinner strolls, tourists mugging for selfies, and couples posing for their engagement or wedding photos.

Now, more than seventy years later, the historic neighborhood is at risk again. Time and traffic have taken their toll on the highway, and in 2018 it was determined to be in dire need of significant repairs. To fix it, the New York City Department of Transportation proposed closing the promenade for six years and building a temporary highway in its place while the old highway was repaired. In response, the BHA mobilized the community to fight the NYC DOT's plan. During this fraught time the Brooklyn Heights Designer Showhouse was launched to raise funds to support these efforts.

To people outside the design world, show houses seem little more than a fun opportunity to snoop around grand homes they wouldn't ordinarily get to go inside, and to maybe steal a few decorating ideas. But to people inside the design world, show houses are a big deal, a chance for established designers to try out fanciful ideas they can't attempt in a usual workaday project, and for emerging designers to gain the kind of exposure that can make a career. Also, because most show houses donate their proceeds to local charitable causes, a swank social event or two is usual, whether an evening of cocktails or a seated dinner, to raise extra funds.

Show houses take place all across the country and are often considered a major social event of the year, attended by local philanthropists and politicians, and covered in the local press (and even nationally—though, far less so these days, now that so many decorating and design magazines have vanished). In New York, crowds flock to the annual Kips Bay Decorator Show House, which was founded in 1973 by supporters of the Kips Bay Boys & Girls Club to raise much-needed funds for after-school and enrichment programs. Each year, as many as fifteen thousand guests pass through the doors of whatever luxury Manhattan home has been selected to see makeovers by scores of the city's top designers, to the tune of over $17 million raised since its founding. The event has proven so successful that in 2017 a second location was added, in Palm Beach, Florida, in partnership with the Boys & Girls Clubs of Palm Beach County.

Tonight's show house takes place in a house that dates back to the late 1700s—according to Truman Capote's famous 1959 essay, "Brooklyn Heights: A Personal Memoir." After opening with the still-resonant lines "I live in Brooklyn. By choice," Capote describes the neighborhood he lived in while writing *Breakfast at Tiffany's*, including this stately gray-shingled home on Pineapple Street: "I'm not much acquainted with the proper history of the Heights. However, I *believe* (but please don't trust me) that the oldest house, the oldest still extant and functioning, belongs to our back-yard neighbors, Mr. and Mrs. Philip Broughton. A silvery gray, shingle-wood Colonial shaded by trees robustly leafed, it was built in 1790, the home of a sea captain."

I have walked by this house countless times. A rarity in a neighborhood dominated by brownstone row houses, this freestanding structure is forty feet wide and twenty-five feet deep, with an Italianate-style bracketed cornice and entry portico that were added when the roof was raised in the 1800s. As a frequent gawker, I can vouch that it looks exactly the same today as when Capote immortalized it; the only details he neglected to mention are the black-painted window shutters and the white trim. I always longed to see inside.

Here's my chance. After checking in with two young women helming a ticket table on the sidewalk, I walk up the front stairs and into the entry hall, where I'm greeted by a black-clad waiter carrying a silver tray of wineglasses. I politely nod my refusal (I'm on the clock, after all), accept a goat-cheese canapé from a different server, and start making my way to the back of house, which is easier said than done. I'd made sure to arrive early, but already the house is crowded floor to rafters with all kinds of elegantly dressed people. Talking enthusiastically, they move from room to room, taking in the many varied designs.

Finally, I find the kitchen, where Whitney and Amanda are surrounded by a small crowd of eager onlookers. When designers are invited to take part in a show house, they are asked to list the top three rooms they'd like to redecorate, in order of preference. JPL's top choice was the kitchen, and the firm was thrilled to get it.

The medium-size kitchen, suited to the original bones of the house, is not the sort of enormous, open-plan kitchen you tend to find in high-end city apartments. The back wall curves outward and features an old-fashioned bay window that looks out onto the patio below. When JPL inherited the room, it had an ordinary, farmhouse-inspired feel, with oak cabinets, simple blue-and-white tiles, a silver stove, and an oak-plank floor. A late twentieth-century makeover, most likely.

At first, JPL thought it was only allowed to change the paint and hardware—until it was told to gut the entire room and start from scratch. Show houses are a chance not only for designers to showcase their work, but for manufacturers and furniture makers to display their wares. The French paint company Ressource agreed to be JPL's paint sponsor, the New Jersey–based architectural woodwork and metalwork studio Cottingham LTD donated the cabinetry, and the Connecticut-based general contractor Apex Projects LLC installed everything. The rest—furniture, window treatments, upholstery, artworks—was donated as well from various vendors.

The makeover happened quickly, in just under five weeks. The old cabinets were ripped out and replaced with modern seamless white cabinetry. The old appliances were hauled off so that new ones could take their place, all of which—the refrigerator, apron-front farmhouse sink, and stove—are a chic matte black (along with the countertops). JPL covered the walls from floor to ceiling with textured Spanish terra-cotta tile from Walker Zanger, a ceramics-and-tile company founded in New York in 1962. Instead of tearing out the floor, JPL painted it white, then worked with a decorative painter to add a geometric pattern inspired by an early-1900s sketch by textile artist Anni Albers. A grid of gray, yellow, and red rectangles of varying sizes, the result is so perfectly executed that at first I mistook it for inlaid floor tiles.

JPL painted the bay window trim glossy teal and created a breakfast nook by adding a custom curved bench uphol-stered in an ornate black-and-rust pattern by Décors Bar-bares. A 1960s vintage Osvaldo Borsani dining table with scalloped edges, and simple bistro-style curtains in a Muriel

Brandolini fabric covering the bottom third of the windows, bring a sweet, cozy feel.

"Our goal wasn't a lofty, grand show kitchen, but rather something that felt warm, approachable, and homey," JPL told *domino* when the room was featured on the magazine's website.

AFTER TAKING A TOUR of the show house, I stepped outside. Standing out back in the garden, every window of the house aglow, the darkening sky threatening rain, I thought of French philosopher Gaston Bachelard's famous book from 1958, *The Poetics of Space*. He noted that extreme weather events, which wreak so much disaster, downing power lines and tearing limbs from trees, can also be experienced as quite beautiful if one is snug inside. While sleet lashes the windows, and cold air gusts through the floorboards, one remembers a home's most essential, fundamental role: to shelter.

What I love about that observation is how it speaks to the necessity of interiors as spaces that not only protect us, but also feel good. That is, shelter and coziness are two separate phenomena. One is a fundamental human necessity, the other a fortunate sensation. When the two are combined—when someone makes an effort to make a house a home—we are better able to appreciate our experience, for good and for ill.

That evening, and for many days after, I wondered if I, too, could strike out on a second career and become an interior designer.

FURTHER READING

The following books provide various perspectives on the world of interior design, including history, reference, and social criticism.

Love Affairs with Houses by Bunny Williams. New York: Harry N. Abrams, 2019.

    In her most recent book, the reigning doyenne of decorating shares fifteen of her favorite projects, including tips for great design.

History of Interior Design by Jeannie Ireland. New York: Fairchild Books, 2018.

    This comprehensive survey of architecture, interiors, and furniture that ranges from ancient times to the present is a treasure trove of fascinating information.

New York School of Interior Design—Home: The Foundations of Enduring Space by Ellen S. Fisher. New York: Clarkson Potter, 2018.

From one of America's first interior design schools, an education on everything you need to know about how to decorate a space, from color theory principles to choosing furniture.

The Interior Design Reference & Specification Book by Chris Grimley and Mimi Love. Beverly, MA: Rockport Publishers, 2018.

A thorough, straightforward guidebook to the fundamentals of interior design that offers updated data on sustainability guidelines and online sources for interiors-related research.

Interior Design Master Class: 100 Lessons from America's Finest Designers on the Art of Decoration, edited by Carl Dellatore. New York: Rizzoli, 2016.

This beautifully illustrated collection of essays by one hundred of today's top interior designers, both established and emerging, ranges from "Collecting" to "Layering" to "Inspiration."

Residential Interior Design: A Guide to Planing Spaces by Maureen Mitton and Courtney Nystuen. Hoboken, NJ: John Wiley & Sons, 2016.

Packed with drawings, photographs, and information,

the third edition of this industry-standard reference for interior design emphasizes human-space interaction, including updated information about accessibility and "aging in place."

The Poetics of Space by Gaston Bachelard. Maria Jolas, trans. New York: Penguin Classics, 2014.

Since it was first published in 1958, this lyrical, philosophical work combines poetry and art to explore the hold that domestic spaces have on our very consciousness.

Edith Wharton at Home: Life at the Mount by Richard Guy Wilson. New York: The Monacelli Press, 2012.

An architectural historian's guide to the country estate designed floor to ceiling by one of America's preeminent novelists.

The Great Lady Decorators: The Women Who Defined Interior Design, 1870–1955 by Adam Lewis. New York: Rizzoli, 2010.

Elsie de Wolfe, Rose Cummings, Dorothy Draper— these are just a few of the pioneering decorators who are given their due in this gorgeously produced social history of the birth of interior design as we know it.

Parish-Hadley: Sixty Years of American Design by Sister Parish, Albert Hadley, and Christopher Petkanas. New York: Little, Brown & Co, 1995.

Personal reminiscences, lavishly illustrated, from two of America's most legendary interior designers.

ABOUT THE AUTHOR

Kate Bolick's first book, *Spinster: Making a Life of One's Own*, was a *New York Times* bestseller and a *New York Times* Notable Book of 2015. Formerly executive editor of *domino* magazine, she writes for a variety of publications here and abroad, including the *New York Times*, the *Wall Street Journal*, *ELLE*, and *Vogue*, and serves as the Design Crimes columnist for *ELLE Decor*. She teaches nonfiction writing at Columbia and New York Universities, speaks frequently at colleges and conferences, and has appeared on the *Today* show, CNN, MSNBC, and numerous NPR programs across the country.